GAMES, GRAPHICS AND SOUNDS

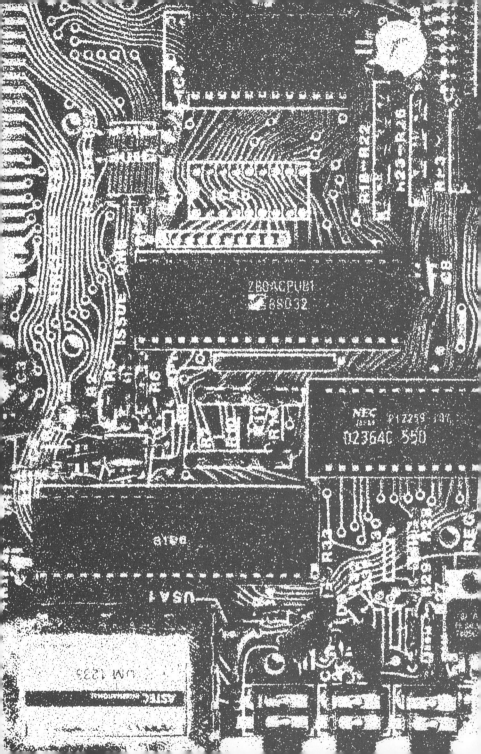

GAMES, GRAPHICS AND SOUNDS

Susan Curran
Ray Curnow

A Fireside Book

Published by Simon & Schuster, Inc.
New York

The authors
Susan Curran is co-author, with Gordon Pask, of *Micro Man:
The Revolution of a Species*, with Horace Mitchell of *Office
Automation: An Essential Management Strategy* and with
Ray Curnow, her husband, of *The Silicon Factor* and *The
Penguin Computing Book*. She was a major contributor to and
editor of the BBC's *The Computer Book*. Susan Curran is
Director of Probit Consultancies and has a specialist
knowledge of user aspects of microcomputers.

Ray Curnow is Professor of Systems Sciences at City
University, London, and an information technology consultant.
He was responsible for structuring and developing the BBC
series *The Computer Programme*, which has been televized
several times. Among the many books he has written are *The
Silicon Factor – Coming to Terms with Microelectronics,
The Future with Microelectronics* and, with Susan Curran,
The Penguin Computing Book. He is currently Director of
Probit Consultancies and a computer advisor to several
multinational microtechnology corporations.

The Clear and Simple Home Computer Series
was conceived, edited and designed by
Frances Lincoln Limited,
Apollo Works, 5 Charlton Kings Road
London NW5 2SB, England.

A Fireside Book
Published by Simon & Schuster, Inc.
Simon & Schuster Building, Rockefeller Center
1230 Avenue of the Americas, New York, New York 10020

FIRESIDE and colophon are registered trademarks of
Simon & Schuster, Inc.

Simultaneously published in Great Britain by
W H Smith & Son Limited under the Windward imprint.

Printed and bound by Hazell, Watson and Viney, England.

1 2 3 4 5 6 7 8 9 10

Library of Congress Catalog Card Number 83-81721

ISBN: 0-671-49444-9

Contents

Introduction

More and more people are taking the plunge and buying a home computer. What do they use them for? Overwhelmingly, they use them to play games.

Maybe that is not how you intend to use your own home computer. You would not be alone in thinking that. Most people, when asked why they are buying a home computer, say that they want to teach themselves and their children about computing. In fact, it is estimated that around eighty percent of all buyers give education as their main reason for buying a computer. It is just as well, then, that games are educational.

Games are also fun, of course. Whatever sort of game you most enjoy playing – fast games or slow, thought-provoking games that go on for hours, games of action or games of strategy, word games or games with mathematics – you will certainly find some computer games that will appeal to you (and probably some that you can hardly tear yourself away from).

Some games are designed specially for learning, to teach children or adults geometry, spelling, foreign languages, history, geography and so on. Other games are less obviously educational, but can still teach you a lot. For example, playing Space Invaders gives you practice in coordinating your movements, in planning strategies (and finding out if they work!) and, perhaps most important of all, in getting used to using computers.

Buying a few games, then, when you first get your new computer is a pretty good idea. They will help you to familiarize yourself with the keyboard and the operating commands, and later they will give you a well-earned break from computing the household accounts or whatever.

In this book, we plan to introduce you to the whole exciting field of computer entertainment: what sort of games are available; what you can expect to find in those cellophane-wrapped cassettes, disks or cartridges; which games give the best value for money? We will answer all these questions for you. At the same time, we will show you how you can learn about computing by writing your own games programs, or adapting those you find in magazines and books. We will also be giving you some programs to help get you started.

Which computer? If you already have a computer or have decided what computer to buy, then that is fine. All personal computers can be used for playing games. If, however, you have not yet made your choice, we will tell you about some of the features you should look for. We will also tell you about peripherals, that is extra equipment such as joysticks and light pens, that you can use with your computer to make game-playing even more enjoyable.

We had to choose a particular computer to write our programs for. This is for two main reasons. First, because each home computer has its own special games, graphics and sounds features and we could not include in a book of this size as detailed an account as we would like on how the programs are written for several different machines. Second, because the home computer market is in constant flux, and any selection of machines would be of limited value and therefore unsatisfactory. By looking in detail at programming strategies and how we construct and write games programs for a single machine, you will be able to understand fully what we did and for what reasons.

We wrote our programs in Microsoft BASIC, the most easy-to-follow and least idiosyncratic form of the language. It is the language that is used on the TRS-80 Color Computer, the Dragon 32, the Video Genie and many other popular home computers. The programs are written for the Dragon, but will run with little or no change on machines such as the TRS-80 Color Computer with Extended BASIC. Even if you have a different machine, we give you enough explanation to adapt the programs to run on your computer without much trouble.

Do you know anything about computing? Possibly not. You may have learned a little at school or college. You may have bought some computer magazines (and perhaps found them difficult to understand). Or you may be a complete beginner.

However much or however little you know, you

Space Invaders in your living room!

A home computer system made up of the computer, a TV set and a pair of joysticks – plus, of course, the right games programs – will give you and your family many hours of amusement. If fast-action games such as Space Invaders – shown here – are not to your taste, there are plenty of other kinds of games to choose from, and you can dispense with the joysticks.

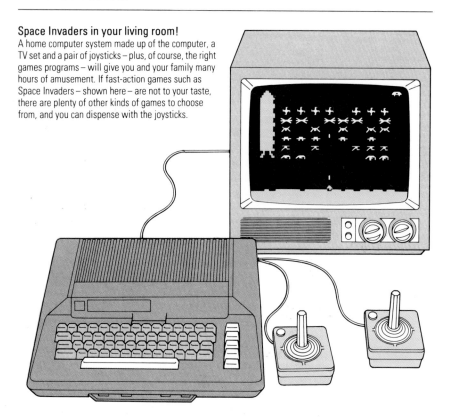

should find plenty in this book to interest and entertain you. If you are a novice, you will find information about choosing and using ready-written games, whether on cassette, disk or cartridge, or listed in magazines ready for you to type into the computer. If you already know something about programming in BASIC, the most popular language for home computers, then you will learn how to put your knowledge to work in writing games and graphics programs.

We will not be teaching you BASIC from scratch. There is too much else to tell you! Most of our programs are written simply, however, and if you have picked up a little BASIC from your computer manual, or from a first book on BASIC, you should have no difficulty in following the listings and our general suggestions on program development and writing.

Games on the home computer

If you are used to playing arcade-type games such as Asteroids and Pac-Man, you may find that it takes a little while to get used to their home-computer cousins. The ideas are the same, but the details will often vary as some home computers are not as powerful (in terms of memory capacity) as the arcade machines and most have been produced not only for game-playing but also for small-business and educational applications. The best home-computer games, however, are every bit as much fun to play as the original versions, if less spectacular.

If you are an expert at chess, backgammon or other board games, then you may well be able to find a computer version to suit you. The same is true of adventure games like Dungeons and Dragons.

Graphics, color and sound

Many home computers can produce excellent pictures, diagrams and line drawings. Quite a few of them can handle color, if you use them with a color television. We will be looking at graphics, not only because lots of games use them, but because they are interesting in their own right. Some of the programs we include are not games programs but special graphics routines designed to show you the sort of displays you can produce using simple BASIC commands.

Sound is important, too. Most computers can produce a range of simple 'beeps' to enliven games and add realism. Some of them can do better, and allow you to produce recognizable tunes. We will explain how all this is done, and how you can use these features yourself in a variety of programs.

That takes care of the introduction. Now let's make a start and see what computers can really do for you!

1 A short history of computer games

How did computer games begin? Computer buffs would say that they began with the very first computers, back in the 1940s. To people who work with computers, playing with a computer is a game, even when it is being done for a serious purpose! Likewise, inventors regard designing computers as a game. Ever since there have been large computers to play with, computer programmers have been playing games with their machines, and this goes back thirty years or more, depending upon your definition of a computer. Whenever there were a few free seconds of computer time – and these early computers cost so much and were used so intensively that a few seconds at a time were all that could be hoped for – the programmers and operators would slip in a 'fun' program or two to liven things up.

What were these 'fun' programs? Perhaps the favorites were computer drawings of Snoopy, naked ladies, the Mona Lisa, and other illustrations that can be made using the letters of the alphabet typed in different combinations. The programmers would feed in a set of punched cards telling the computer what to do, and out came the pictures on the computer's line-printer. An example of this early 'computer art' – a portrait of Charles Babbage – is shown opposite.

There is no particularly elaborate programming behind most of these: just a lot of hard work! The artist worked out what he wanted the computer to draw, letter by letter, and then gave the machine the instructions for it to get on with the job.

Drawings were particularly handy because they were suited to the pace of that generation of computers. When you fed in a bunch of cards (rather than typed on a keyboard) and then had to wait for the computer to process them and type out its results on a line-printer, you could hardly expect to play fast-action games like Asteroids and Breakout!

Computer art

Above left, an engraving of Charles Babbage (1791–1871), one of the pioneers of the modern computer. Above right, a line-printer version of the engraving. The line-printer image was produced by a mainframe computer using a set of punched cards (one card is shown left) to program the machine. It is not really a computer picture – there is no such thing – just a pattern of overprinted letters put out on a line-printer.

Chess   Chess-playing programs were also developed very early, from the late 1940s and early 1950s. They took a lot of planning and could not just be done at odd moments. Getting a computer to play chess was a long, slow business, and much of the research was carried out full time in universities. Researchers devoted a great deal of time to the game of chess because it is such a good example of a complicated thought process. By 'teaching' a computer chess, they were learning how to teach the computer intelligent behavior in general.

It took a long while before computers became any good at chess. The first computer chess game was, arguably, one played on a computer called Maniac 1, in Los Alamos, New Mexico, in 1956, in which, to make its task simpler, the machine used a board with only thirty-six squares instead of the normal sixty-four. It took around twelve minutes for the computer to make each move, and its playing strength was reckoned to be comparable to that of a human who had played about twenty games – a raw beginner, in fact!

The following year, a more powerful computer, an IBM 704, was programmed to play to the finish the first 'real' game of computer chess on a full-sized board. The program was more than ten times as long as the earlier one, but the result was still no better than an average amateur player could manage.

Even today, the best players can beat even the best chess programs. Nevertheless, game theory – the study of strategies for planning out and winning a game – has steadily developed, and now chess programs much more powerful than the expensively developed early efforts can be bought for a few dollars, to run on even the cheapest home computers. They are good, too: most of them have several levels of play, so that they can give a worthwhile game to everyone from the beginner to the expert.

Other traditional games, such as checkers, were also used in early research. Because these are less complicated than chess, a well-programmed computer can always work out the best possible move, and will beat the human being every time – unless the programmer takes pity on the player, and instructs the computer to make the occasional mistake.

Computer chess

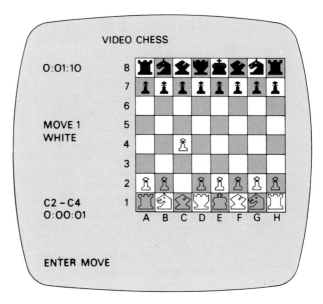

Today's chess programs contain a wealth of chess theory upon which the computer can draw, including numerous ways of playing the opening stages of the game, with some set variations running many moves deep. In the display shown here, the computer, playing White, has taken one second to choose to open the game by advancing a pawn two squares, from C2 to C4. This is the English Opening.

Adventure games

Perhaps the real breakthrough came, however, when, instead of getting computers to play long-established games, programmers started to invent games specially for computers. This new generation of games made use of the computer's endless patience and its phenomenal ability to remember information and to combine that information in all sorts of ways. They were called 'adventure' games.

In an adventure game the player travels through a world of adventures created on the computer. To play, you tell the computer where you want to go – north, south, east or west – and what you want to do. Every time you make a move, the computer describes where you have arrived at and what is happening there. A player may encounter strange beings, be taught magic spells, find treasure, or be attacked and robbed. There is a goal – treasure to be found, or knowledge to be gained – but often the goal takes a long time to reach, and few if any players ever do reach it. If you play over a whole weekend, you still may hardly have started on the quest. To make progress, you have to learn the rules of the game (they are not spelled out to you in advance), map out the world the computer leads you through, and generally put in a lot of time and effort.

Noncomputer adventure games have been developed, using human guides instead of computers; but adventuring is essentially a game of the computer age, and one that is ideally suited to the computer's abilities. In strange and sometimes frightening ways, it echoes the uncertainty most of us feel about our relationship with the computer. Does it really understand us, or is there 'nobody there'? Will it take over our lives? Adventure games have certainly taken over the lives of plenty of addicts.

One of the first adventure games, called simply Adventure, was developed by computer experts in the USA in the late 1970s. Tracy Kidder's *The Soul of a New Machine* gives a vivid account of the 'midnight programmers' who stayed on after working hours to play Adventure, and of how it was used as the acid test to see if a new computer was working properly.

Serious uses of computers have often been adapted to provide computer entertainment. Take, for instance, computer simulation of driving a car, or flying an airplane, or even controlling a spaceship. Many training programs include elaborate computer simulations, designed to give the learner a taste of what is in store, without risking lives or damage to expensive equipment. At the same time, cheaper simulations are also available purely for entertainment. You can land on the moon, or drive a race car, all in your own living room, taking full advantage of the research that went into the 'proper' versions.

Computer-aided design and manufacturing have also had their spin-offs. The computer systems used in the design of complicated mechanical parts, or of buildings, and often in the control of the machines that make them are a major investment. Obviously, the 'draw-it-yourself'

'Flight Simulator'

The main display generally looks like this. At the top of the screen is a simplified view from the cockpit; below is shown the dashboard. The various dials and indicators respond to your 'handling' of the controls, just as they would on a real aircraft. To fly the plane, you simply type in your commands at the keyboard (or use a joystick). You can usually find out from the screen display map where you are in relation to airstrips and other landmarks. If the worst comes to the worst, there is a spectacular crash sequence that you will be able to enjoy – in total safety!

program you can buy for your computer will not be nearly as sophisticated as today's most elaborate systems, but it is a fair copy of the sort of system and program that were expensive only a few years ago. Your home computer has the kind of computing power and memory which, until recently, only the largest machines possessed.

Video games Much of the work that has gone into today's computer games was done on large, mainframe computers, in the days before home computers existed. There are, however, other ancestors of your computer game cartridge. One of these is the video game.

'Pinball' machines, arcade games using mechanical springs and electric sensors, have been around for decades. In the early 1970s, we began to see the emergence of their electronic counterparts. These new games had a screen like a television screen, and the player used 'joystick'-type controls to move a bat, or fire a streak of light.

The father of video machines was an American called Nolan Bushnell. He developed a prototype of a video game called Computer Space, a battle between a flying saucer and a spaceship, back in 1971. Compared to today's elaborate games, it was extremely simple. Bushnell followed it up with two other classic games: video tennis, where two players hit a ball from side to side across the screen, and Breakout, the game in which you knock down a wall, brick by brick. Bushnell went on to found Atari, one of the largest of the video games companies.

At first, these simple video games were found in cafés and penny arcades. Later, versions for use in the home were developed. The first TV game was produced by Magnavox in 1972. It was an elaborate affair which used colored 'overlays', each bearing a game board in the form of a cut-out. The player set up a game by sticking an overlay across the screen, and then the computer produced a single, movable dot of light which could 'fire' at the different targets. TV tennis was simpler, and took off on a much greater scale. In 1975, Atari produced a new version, called Pong. The Pong computer could play only Pong – ping-pong, that is – but its successors managed to play a variety of simple bat-and-ball-type games.

By the late 1970s, television games were all the rage. There were many TV games machines on sale – small computers, but computers that could play only the games they had been programmed to play. They did not have the ability to accept programs written by the user, using a language such as BASIC. We call them 'dedicated' computers, in contrast to general-purpose computers like today's popular home computers.

While television games began to copy the early arcade games, the penny arcades moved on to greater things. Perhaps the greatest of all was Space Invaders, the game which a Japanese company, Taito, launched on an unsuspecting world in 1978.

Breakout had never been a serious rival to pinball machines: its tiny, TV-like screen could not compare with their bright displays. Space Invaders was an altogether different story. The screen was brighter, and colored, of course and even the box that housed it was brash and startling. Soon, Space Invaders and other games like it – games such as Defender, Galaxian, Asteroids, Pac-Man – were sweeping the world.

These arcade games are also controlled by dedicated computers, but much more powerful ones than those in the early TV-game sets. Only today, a few years after Space Invaders made its first appearance, are we starting to see home-computer games that really com-

Hand-held computer games

Like arcade games machines, most hand-held electronic games sets are 'dedicated' computers – that is, they are designed to play a game and do nothing more. A microcomputer can do very much more, and play many different games besides.

pare in quality with these early arcade games. Meanwhile, of course, the arcade games have gone on to new heights of complexity and sophistication that home computers cannot yet match.

While Space Invaders was taking the arcades of the world by storm, a much greater variety of dedicated games began to appear on the home front. Many of these were not TV games: they were hand-held versions of the early video games, with their own built-in displays. Other uses, too, were made of computer power for fun or entertainment. There were robot toys, fitted with computers, that could talk to children, and other computers that could help them with their spelling.

The first hand-held game machines played only a single game, but today some versions can take cartridges that enable them to play a variety of games. Each cartridge contains the program for a particular game, locked into its memory circuits. All these games were made possible by the explosion in computer technology which led, most importantly, to the appearance of the first home computers.

Home computers

The very first cheap computers, such as the Altair which came out in the USA in 1975, were not really 'home' computers in today's sense. They were hobby machines, which electronics enthusiasts, who naturally got a kick out of making the computer actually *do* something, would put together in their spare time. Much of the fun, for them, lay in making the machine, and tinkering with its hardware. There were not many ready-written games waiting to be played on these home-made masterpieces: it was strictly a do-it-yourself enterprise.

Even when the amazingly popular Sinclair ZX80 and Timex 1000 (ZX81) computers appeared, in 1980 and 1981, they were sold in kit form as well as ready-assembled. Many of their early buyers wanted to find out how computers worked, not to play games. Only slowly did the kit sales decline, until, eventually, the kits were abandoned and just the finished machines sold.

As the home computer market has developed, more and more people who know nothing at all about electronics or computing have decided to buy home computers. They do not want to spend their evenings messing around with soldering irons: they want to play games! The computer industry has become increasingly aware of this fact. Today, it is taken for granted that buying a computer is just a start. Once you have bought your machine, you are likely to spend at least as much again purchasing games for it.

At first, games came only on cassette tapes. They were fairly cheap, but not easy to handle. Now, more and more ready-written games programs are in cartridge form instead. The cartridge contains a block of computer memory, in which the programs are already written. This memory is a ROM (read-only memory), not read-write, or random access, like the memory you get in add-on RAM packs. All the user has to do is to link the memory circuitry to the main computer circuitry (which you do by pushing in the cartridge!) and switch on.

Cassettes and cartridges
Computer games are commonly available on cassette and cartridge. Cartridges are better, but they can be much more expensive.

Games and graphics programs

Why are people buying general-purpose home computers instead of the ever more sophisticated games machines? After all, some of the money you spend on a home computer goes into the features that make it general-purpose – such as its keyboard – and so, if playing games is your only object, it is not quite as good value as the games-only machines. There is always the knowledge, however, that you can, if you wish, do other things with it too. You can buy other types of ready-written program, like home accounts programs, business management programs or teach-yourself programs, and, of course, you can write your own programs for everything from running a model train set to doing geography homework.

We will be looking at writing games and graphics programs later in the book. Many people find that writing the programs is just as much fun as playing the games themselves. But unless you are a really expert programmer the games you write for yourself cannot hope to match those you buy prewritten. The quickest action games are not written in the easy-to-learn BASIC language, but in the computer's machine code – that is, a sequence of 0s and 1s – which is not nearly so easy to handle.

Of course, you can always bridge the gap between cartridges, cassettes and disks, and pencil and paper, by buying computer magazines and books and trying out the program listings they give you. If you have the time to type the listings in, they can save you a lot of money compared with the games you buy. We will be looking at this possibility, too, later in the book.

Your home computer is a very powerful machine, and it can, if you give it good programs, play an enormous variety of exciting and thought-provoking games with you. You may be disappointed if you expect it to turn into a penny arcade: the dedicated arcade machines are always likely to be one step ahead of the general-purpose computer games. On the other hand, if you concentrate on what your machine *can* do, you will find that there is more than enough to keep you happy, playing – and learning too!

Types of computer games

What sorts of computer games can you buy, or program for yourself? In this chapter, we will be looking at some of the features offered by games, and at ways of identifying those games that provide what you are looking for.

Familiar games

Lots of computer games, of course, are old favorites reworked for the computer. Board games, card games and pencil-and-paper games have all been adapted for the small screen. In fact, whatever your favorite game – from darts to backgammon – the chances are that someone, somewhere, has written a computer program to play it with you.

Why play a game like chess or Hangman on the computer when you can play it at home with little or no equipment, anyway? These are some of the advantages:

The computer is always ready to play. Except for solitaire and patience (and yes, there are computer versions of those), most games need at least two players. If there is nobody at hand who wants to play your favorite game with you, it can be nice to know that the computer is always ready and willing. It never gets fed up before you do, even when it has a run of rotten luck!

The computer will do all the dirty work for you. Nobody wants to keep the score? No problem: the computer will do the job – and shuffle the cards and deal the pack.

The computer will not cheat. An adventure program may drive you mad; a chess program may expose the weaknesses in your play and infuriate you; but you can be certain that no program will cheat you. It keeps to the rules, and may warn you if *you* try to break them.

The computer is a good teacher. Not only will it make sure you remember the rules of chess correctly: many programs will also suggest moves to you, if you are stuck for ideas. If you really have worked yourself into a hole, you can often change places with the computer, and enjoy being on the winning side for a change!

Familiar games

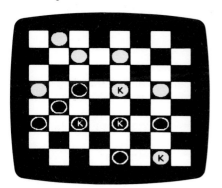

Good as a computer is at chess, it is even better at checkers (above). Because checkers is a simpler game, there are fewer possibilities to calculate, which means that the computer's ability to look ahead counts for very much more. A good game for changing sides once you find yourself taking a pasting!

There are many commercial versions of Hangman (below) available, or you can write your own program for it if you prefer. Traditionally, Hangman has been a guessing game to do with words, but some of the variations that have been developed for computers use figures and numbers, and are aimed at improving arithmetical skills.

Though there are many computer games that derive from or have noncomputer equivalents, certain games lead the pack in terms of popularity and what is available for the computer. This is partly because some games are easier to program than others (you will not find many computer bridge games, for instance, while there are lots of versions of simpler, highly logical games like Gobang), and partly because some are easier to play on the computer than others. It is difficult to imagine why anyone would want to play darts with a computer, for example, though quite a good version is available if you care to try it.

These are some of the long-established games which are now available in computer-program form:

Chess Needs no introduction.

Checkers Simpler than chess, but still a good way of passing a rainy afternoon.

Backgammon The computer will 'gamble' with you after a fashion, but some people still feel that without real money at stake, the game loses a lot.

Blackjack Even more of a gambling game: it is better if there are two or more players, with the computer as banker and 'umpire'.

Tick-tac-toe Both the conventional kind and a nifty three-dimensional version are available.

Hangman The good versions have a wide range of words to guess, of different levels of difficulty, and/or let you feed in your own.

Dice and *Dominoes* Lots of variations are available.

Mastermind The classic 'guess my hand' game.

Countertake A logical game which is harder than it looks.

Go, Othello Also, a wide variety of other less common board games.

You will find programs for some of the simpler games later on in the book.

Hand-and-eye games   Television tennis and ping-pong, Space Invaders, and the many other arcade-type games we mentioned briefly in the last chapter all come under the general heading of hand-and-eye coordination games. That is not to suggest that strategy does not come into them – in the better ones it counts for a lot – but the main interest is in coordinating your actions so as to hit the ball or blow up the alien.

The simplest coordination games are *very* simple. Either the computer holds the target still, and it is your job to move your bat or rocket launcher into position, or the computer moves the target (as in a shooting gallery) and you fire at it from a fixed position. In the more complicated versions, you and the computer both make moves. In some space games, for instance, you have to steer your spaceship through a region strewn with moving asteroids or enemy ships.

It is easy to tire of very simple hand-and-eye games. Once you have mastered them, the interest soon wains. All but the very simplest home-programmed efforts, however, offer you several levels of play: the game speeds up, the bat gets smaller, the obstacles get larger or there are more of them. It is a good idea to select a game in which you can choose the level of difficulty from the start, so that you do not have to work through the 'easy' levels each time, before reaching something that presents a challenge. Players' abilities vary a great deal and if there are several levels to choose from, you are

Hand-and-eye games

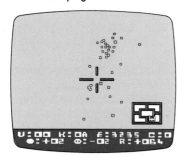

Star Raiders

In a typical space game, the aliens move in a fairly predictable pattern, so that the player then only has to position his or her own craft correctly before letting loose with the fire button. But sometimes the aliens shoot back – often blindly, but in some of the better versions they can get you in their sights before retaliating!

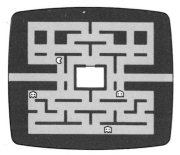

Pac-Man

There are lots of different versions of this game (all with different names). Basically, the idea is to guide the Pac-Man around the maze, scoring points for eating fruit and energizers and avoiding the monsters that inhabit the maze until you are ready to gobble them up.

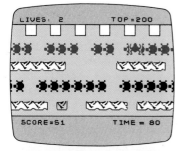

Frogger

Here, the object is to help the frog reach the safety of the lily pads, avoiding the dangers presented by various natural phenomena and the trappings of human civilization. You have control over the movement of the frog, but nothing else.

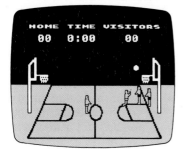

Basketball

Not quite the Harlem Globetrotters, but an exciting game for all that! Movement on the screen is controlled by joysticks, and you can either play against the computer or a human opponent. Basketball is just one of the many ball games that are being played on the small screen, even when there is no televized fixture for that day!

more likely to find one that suits you.

What features distinguish one game from another? These are some of the things to check on:

Can more than one person play? Are there options to suit one, two or more players, or is there a fixed number of players?

If the game is one in which the computer sets up the scene for you, but does not compete against you, as in Breakout (where the computer builds the wall, delivers the balls, but does not try to hit the balls), it is a good idea to find someone to play against, at least occasionally. Trying to beat your own best score is not as much fun as trying to beat somebody else! You can always take turns, but it is better still if you play simultaneously, competing to see who hits the asteroids first, say. Many computer games are set up to allow you to do this. Some games give you the option of either playing against the computer, or playing against another person.

Is the game the same every time? Some people find it dull if, say, the space invader 'saucer' repeatedly scores 15 points every second time. Once they have cracked the pattern, they lose interest. Others are happy to accept a predictable pattern, and get upset if they cannot find one!

What is the display like? A lot of the interest in these games comes from the graphic display that appears on the screen. Is the subject of the game one that appeals to you? (The same basic ideas can turn up in the guise of many different games – space games, mystical 'dragon' games, cowboys and indians, and so on.) Is the display well planned? Do interesting things happen in the game when you are doing well? Or even when you are doing badly? In some versions of 'Meteor Storm', for instance, there's a certain perverse pleasure in failing to blow up the meteors: the explosions they make by themselves are so much more exciting!

Some of these features depend upon the actual game you choose; some, of course, depend upon the particular version of the game you have. We will be looking in more depth at the major differences between good and poor game programs when we consider prewritten software in Chapter 8.

Can you take your time? In some games, you can choose when you make your move. Labyrinth is one of them. You move at your own pace, and there are times when you can take a break without anything disastrous happening. Breakout is quite the opposite. The ball keeps on coming toward your bat, and you have to get there in time. Some people enjoy fast action; others like co-ordination games, but prefer to take them slowly.

Here is a list of some of the hand-and-eye games that are available, together with a brief description of each. The home-computer versions will not be identical to their arcade counterparts, as we explained earlier. Moreover, if they were devised by different companies they will have slightly different names.

Space Invaders The classic arcade game. Many other space games have followed it: Galaxian, Defender and so on. All offer variations on a theme. The player normally has one or more 'bases' at the bottom of the screen, and defends these from the encroaching aliens, which sweep down toward them in waves.

Asteroids Again a space theme, but a little less blood-thirsty. You have to blast the asteroids to pieces before they crush your ship. Many versions also boast enemy spaceships to provide a diversion; often a less 'busy' display than the invader kind of game.

Pac-Man A whole series of bizarre games involving cartoon characters munching their way around their mini-worlds, collecting rewards and avoiding dangers. Simpler versions are also common. One of these is Snake, in which you move a snake around the screen making it eat numbers or characters.

Frogger It may be pushing it to call this an ecology game! It is, however, a gentler game than many of the other arcade games, with the frog having to make its way home by negotiating obstacles such as busy roads and fast-flowing rivers.

Breakout A family of bat-and-ball games, which involves breaking down a wall, brick by brick, as you hit it with the ball. A simple game to program yourself (see our version on page 00).

Football and *Tennis* There is enormous variation in the ways in which real-life ball games are imitated on the screen. In most versions, you control one or more players, competing either against the computer or against another player who controls the opposite team. Other ball games that have been computerized include basketball, squash, pinball, golf, tournament pool, billiards and baseball.

Simulation games

In one sense, all the video games that imitate real events on the screen are simulations. We will use this heading, however, to describe 'what if' games, such as Kingdom and Life.

These games simulate a 'real-life' situation – sometimes a complex one, sometimes a very simple one – which the player is invited to control. In Life, you can be Mother Nature, planning the birth and death of organisms. You can be a king or prime minister ruling the economy and planning taxation policies, in games like Kingdom and Great Britain Limited. You can be a spaceman landing a rocket on the moon in Lunar Lander. The computer asks you to make decisions, and then updates its 'model' using your choices. Will you crash, or will you land safely? Will the country accept your rule, or will you be overthrown? Will your microworld thrive, or will it perish? It is comforting to know that if you do badly, you can always go back and try all over again.

In some of these games, also, much of the attraction lies in the screen display. Some versions of the Life game, for instance, with its simulations of the growth and decay of a group of organisms, can produce very attractive patterns on the screen. In other games, you can see your country being invaded or your land flooded if you do badly. (Another case in which losing can be more fun than winning: disasters are much easier to illustrate than successes!) Certain versions, however, are 'text only'. The computer tells you how you are doing, in words or figures, but without any illustrations.

You may think that the text versions must therefore be the poor relations. Far from it. Some of them use up so much of the computer's memory to hold the complexities of their model that there is none left for dramatic screen displays. The appeal may be different, but for some people it is just as great.

Adventure games

We talked briefly about adventure games in the last chapter. They are, if you like, a natural extension of simulations. The difference is that, instead of imitating the real world, most of them create a fantastic world of their own.

The player's aim in an adventure game is not to try to improve the world but to venture through it, solving a problem or finding treasure. Some simple 'quickie' adventure games are rather like answering a riddle: once you get the idea (which can take a while, as adventure games do not go in for detailed instructions), and finish the game, there is nothing left in it for you. (Back you go to the software library, to trade in that game and collect another.) The longer and more complex games extend the idea to what can seem like infinity. They are so elaborate that only a tiny minority of players will ever finish them. The pleasure lies in steadily creeping a little further toward the goal.

How much playing time will you get from an adventure game? This is something that can vary enormously. Dedicated adventurers will enjoy working on the same game for hundreds of hours. A real expert may well exhaust a game in just a few hours, although in the better versions there are usually random elements to maintain the interest. The inexpert may not even manage to get started. Why? Because they spend ages staring at the opening messages, but cannot work out what to do to make something happen. Be warned: in most adventure games not much does happen, at least at first. Be patient. Read any hints that come with the game, or any others you find in reviews of it. Give the computer lots of instructions, including ones not mentioned in the rules; you are unlikely to 'crash' the program, and will probably find that some fanciful suggestion turns out to be just what the program wanted from you!

As with simulations, many adventure games are text-only. The computer's memory space, and the programmer's patience, are taken up with the game content, not with the graphic frills. Slowly, though, pictorial adventure games are coming onto the market. Some of the versions now available on floppy disks, which have more memory space to play with, are truly elaborate, with new pictures to illustrate each new location the

Playing adventure games

Not all adventure games boast pictures, but some of those that do have really amazing ones! The best programs are on disk. On cassette, you're more likely to get cartoon characters and an impressionistic background. They are usually just stills, which are there to admire – you don't control anything in them. Vital in adventure games is the text, for which a 'window' is normally provided at the bottom of the screen, as shown here.

adventurer reaches or situation he finds himself in.

Some adventure games are 'real time': things can happen even without your giving the computer any input. (There you are in the castle, ruminating in the Hall of Kings, when suddenly a message appears: 'The nine-headed hydra has turned up and is about to eat you!') One feature to look for in these games is what is known as a 'quiet' instruction: an instruction that freezes the state of the game while you go off to make a cup of coffee or whatever. Otherwise, you risk having to go back to the beginning each time you return to the game because you discover you have been killed off in your absence!

Once again, it is a good idea to choose a subject that appeals to you. There are mythological adventure games, based on the adventures of Ulysses, Jason or other well-known characters. There are games based on books like *The Hobbit* (or more glamorously, on James Bond). There are historical games, played out in Ancient Rome or the Inca Kingdom; and there are hi-tech versions, set in space stations, as well as thirties-style detective thrillers, and many more besides.

War games are almost a special category by themselves. Board-based war games can be immensely complicated, and their computer equivalents are even more so. The reconstructions of real battles can be educational, but you may find that the software programmer expects you to know quite a lot before you start!

Educational games

As we said earlier, there is a huge variety of educational games. Some are basically educational programs, dressed up in the guise of a game to make the subject more digestible! Many use simple graphics to reward the player for answering a question correctly – give a right answer in the French test and you might launch a rocket, for instance. Others turn the whole exercise into the form of a game: Wordhunt, Wordpower and Hangman games teach spelling; Maths Maze makes mathematics a little more fun to learn.

At the extreme

Longest

The longest computer game we know of is an adventure game written for the Apple II computer: Time Zone, by Ken and Roberta Williams. It covers six floppy disks, and contains over 1400 different pictures!

Highest

Expert players on arcade video games become so good that they can keep a single play going for hours. The highest-ever score at Defender was notched up by a US schoolboy, who kept playing all night (a total of 16 hours 34 minutes), to score around 16 million points!

3 Computer graphics

Let's start this chapter by looking briefly at the way in which the computer handles and stores information about its television or monitor screen display.

You probably know that the computer manipulates numbers and characters (and indeed all the information it handles) by converting them into a binary code, in which they are made up of sequences of the digits 0 and 1. Small home computers normally work with groups of eight 'bits' (short for binary digits), called bytes. Thus the letter A might be coded as the byte 01000001, and the number 15 as 00001111.

Using the same system, the computer stores information about the screen display it is to produce. We can think (very simply) of the computer dividing up the screen into an array of little dots or rectangles, each of which could be either black or white. The computer codes, say, black as 0 and white as 1 and sets aside part of its memory to hold the details of the display pattern. This is called the screen memory, in which every byte stored has its own unique memory location, or address.

Suppose, for instance, the addresses started at number 0020 and the computer held the details row by row in successive memory locations, then the following pattern

0020	0021	0022
01010101	11111111	00000000

would display, at the top left-hand corner of the screen, first a row of alternate black and white squares, then a white line, and then a black line.

If the computer works in color (or can produce shades of gray, on a black and white television or monitor), then it will need to hold information on the exact color each dot is to be. This information, too, can be held as a bit pattern. With three bits, it could fit the code for one of eight colors, like this:

Screen memory map

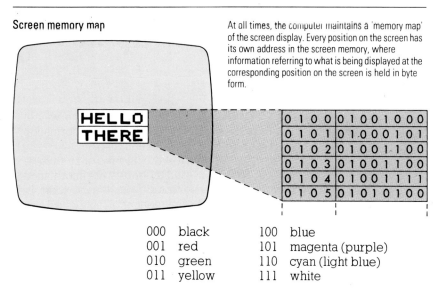

At all times, the computer maintains a 'memory map' of the screen display. Every position on the screen has its own address in the screen memory, where information referring to what is being displayed at the corresponding position on the screen is held in byte form.

000	black	100	blue
001	red	101	magenta (purple)
010	green	110	cyan (light blue)
011	yellow	111	white

In fact, three bits is an awkward number for a machine that works in sets of eight. The computer could more easily use one byte to describe two screen locations, allowing not three but four bits for each. The fourth bit could then extend the range of colors from eight to sixteen, or perhaps describe some other characteristic, such as whether the square is flashing, or extra-bright.

Let's look at an example, assuming 'our' computer uses the color codes we have just given, and puts into the left-hand digit of each group of four a 'flash' code: 0 for 'off', and 1 for 'on'. Then the pattern of three bytes of information we gave earlier would mean:

Two magenta dots, not flashing   (01010101)
Two flashing white dots   (11111111)
Two black dots, not flashing   (00000000)

Fine, you might think: and, indeed, it works very well. What's the problem, then? Simply, the amount of memory that it takes up. A typical low-resolution graphics array might be made up of, say, 64 columns and 32 rows of dots. That's 64 × 32, or 2048 separate little rectangles to describe. Even if the computer fits two of them into each byte of memory, it will still take up 1K (1024 bytes) of memory to describe that one screen full of data. In other words, it would take up *all* the random access memory (RAM) of a very small home computer, like the Timex 1000/Sinclair ZX81, just to store information of a not very detailed color screen display.

Of course, things get even worse when we try to improve the resolution of the picture and fit more dots onto the screen. A home computer high-resolution display might have, say, 256 columns of 192 dots. That's a total of 49,152 dots. If you were to take four bits to describe each of those, you would need 24K of memory – most of the RAM of a fairly powerful home computer.

We can draw two conclusions from this. First, there is going to be a pretty close connection between the size of a computer's RAM and the quality of display it can support – there's no use expecting convincing animated displays in sixteen colors from a tiny computer. Second, there are good reasons why computer manufacturers try to compress the data on screen displays into as little memory space as possible. That way, they can give you the tools to produce good displays, *and* leave some room in RAM for you to enter and run your program!

All computers set aside a section of memory that is used to hold details of the screen display. In some computers, it is quite separate from the rest of the memory. In some, it is only 'temporarily' separated, so that you can tell the computer where to draw the boundary between the 'display memory' and the working memory, depending upon the type of display you want. Many computers *do* set aside a very large chunk of memory, enabling you to describe, dot by dot, one or more displays you want to be created, in just the way we have suggested. (We will be looking later at how you program these details into the computer's memory.) However, virtually all computers employ tricks to allow them to get more display information out of a limited amount of memory space.

The snag is that these tricks make it harder for the programmer. Often they mean that you have to consider the computer's internal workings, when programming graphics, in ways that you don't have to bother about when you are writing other types of program in a high-level language like BASIC. They also impose limitations on how you can set up displays. You may be able to use the full range of the computer's colors only when work-ing at a fairly low resolution; or you may be unable to mix text and graphics on the screen.

Many of these limitations vary from computer to com-puter, and we don't have space to describe exactly how every different model stores graphic information. Instead, we hope that by explaining some of the prin-ciples, we will make it easier for you to understand how your own computer works – or to choose a computer, if you don't yet have one.

Displaying text

Colored rectangles or dots are all very well. But what about characters? How does the computer cope with them?

In fact, every character – letter of the alphabet, number or whatever – that appears on the screen is made up of a pattern of dots. The dot pattern is drawn at high resolution, so that the dots sometimes overlap on a normal TV screen, but the computer knows about them. If it uses, say, an eight-by-ten array to draw its charac-ters, then it might make up A, B and C as shown below.

These are, in fact, characters from one 'character set' on the NewBrain computer, which has four different such sets. Some of them are designed on an eight-by-ten array, some on an eight-by-eight. It is these densities that are used on most small computers.

Whenever you press a character key on your compu-ter, or give the computer a character code using a command like PRINT CHR$(56), the computer has to

Characters on a screen

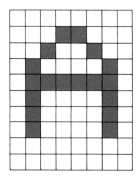 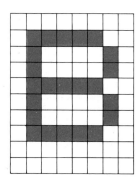 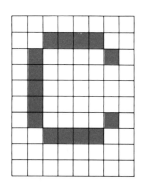

relate the code it uses for the character you want to describe to the pattern of dots it will need to call up to make that character appear on the screen. The computer's 'character generator' normally does this automatically for you, by referring to a set of stored dot-patterns in memory: one for each character in the computer's character set(s). These patterns are stored in read only memory (ROM).

With some computers, however, you can, instead, tell the character generator to get its patterns from a section of RAM that you've set aside for the purpose. Using this device (exactly how it is done varies), you can redefine part or all of the character set, or add new characters to extend the set. We will be looking at them shortly.

When the computer is printing characters on the screen, we think of it as working at low resolution. Of course, the resolution is only low in one sense. The computer uses just as many dots as it does in high-resolution modes, but we think of the display as being divided up into larger rectangles, each of which is made up of an array of dots that can display a character.

How does the computer's memory work in low resolution? For each of these larger rectangles, the computer will need to hold three kinds of information:
– the code for the character it is to display
– the 'background' or 'paper' color
– the 'foreground' or 'ink' color
Different computers have different ways of organizing the memory they use to hold these various types of information. Generally speaking, low resolution takes up less memory than the very high resolutions used for detailed graphics work.

Graphics characters and user-defined characters

It's no trouble for the computer, instead of looking up the code for, say, A, to look up a pattern like the one shown here. This is a graphics character. A computer usually has a predefined set of such patterns, which it can be told to 'draw' just as easily as it can be told to print an alphanumeric character on the screen. Sometimes you can use the normal keys on your keyboard to do this, by first pressing a special 'graphics' key; sometimes you need to give the computer the character code, using a statement like PRINT CHR\$. Either way, with these ready-made characters, you can make the computer draw quite complicated patterns while still working at the low resolution that is normally used for text.

On some computers, you can, as well as using the predefined graphics characters, define your own characters. You might want to plot out a tiny face or a chess piece on the 'character array'. You would then use special commands to give the computer the information it needs to re-create your character. Normally, you tell the computer what 'code' you will be using to refer to the character, and what is the pattern of 1s and 0s for each row in turn of the array. So, to make the little face shown below, you would feed into the memory location holding the data on row 1 the code 00111100 (or the decimal or hexadecimal equivalent of the number that this represents in binary) and so on. Such characters are known as user-defined characters.

Medium and high resolutions

What is high resolution? The answer is relative. High resolution, to the owner of a TRS-80 Color Computer, is 256 × 192 dots. On the Apple II, it is 280 × 192 dots. To the owner of a black-and-white-only NewBrain, it is 640 × 250 dots. To the user of a special computer-aided design system it may be much higher.

In practice, of course, there is a limit to the quality of display that you can expect to receive from a fairly cheap home computer using a domestic television set. There's no point in being able to describe the display you want in fantastic detail if the hardware used to

Defining your own characters

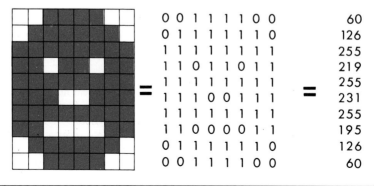

generate the display is not capable of working at a similar level of precision.

As well as describing a degree of resolution, 'high resolution' normally refers to a particular set of commands – in BASIC or another language, such as LOGO – and a particular way of using the screen. High-resolution displays concentrate largely on drawing precise lines, and 'painting' the areas that they enclose (BASIC commands like MOVE, DRAW and PAINT are typical). They are used for 'business graphics' – drawing graphs and bar charts, for instance – and for drawing detailed patterns and pictures. We will see examples of this later in the book.

Sometimes the term medium resolution is used to describe displays that do not work in a 'character' way, but do not offer particularly high resolution either. A typical medium resolution might be double normal text resolution: on the TRS-80 Color Computer, for instance, it is 64 × 32.

Medium-resolution graphics use 'pixels', the term given to little rectangles of color that are larger than the dots of high resolution. The displays are built up by 'setting' pixels to particular colors, rather than by drawing lines as in high resolution. Special BASIC commands are often provided to enable you to SET and RESET individual pixels.

Display modes and windows

Some computers are limited in the ways in which you can mix text and graphics characters, pixel-setting commands and high-resolution commands. The computer works in a variety of 'modes', in which the screen can be described in definite ways, and in which particular commands are used. You tell the computer which mode to use, before programming your display.

Let us look at some examples. On the TRS-80 Color Computer with Extended BASIC and also on the Dragon 32 (two very similar machines), the text and pixel modes are compatible. You can use part of a screen to write messages, and set pixels on and off elsewhere on the screen, using the different 'screen maps' (32 × 16 for text, 64 × 32 for medium resolution) alternately. However, you can't use either of these modes with high-resolution graphics. To get higher

Low, medium and high resolution

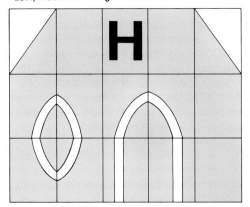

Shown on the left is a typical low-resolution design using text and graphics characters. Graphics characters vary from computer to computer. Those seen in this display are similar to ones found on NewBrain, Sharp and Commodore computers. Medium-resolution graphic displays use pixels (see below). Pixels are double the density of the low-resolution rectangles – that is, there are four times as many within the same area, allowing much greater detail to be displayed.

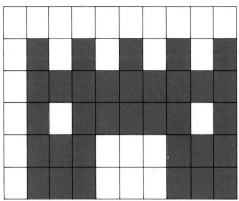

High-resolution graphics (right) allow precise lines to be drawn, rather than just setting pixels to different colors. Areas between lines can be colored in using special BASIC instruction words. Hence the high-resolution mode can display the greatest detail of all, but at the same time uses up more memory than the other modes. Moreover, on some computers high resolution cannot be used together with other modes.

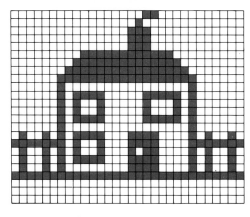

resolution, you tell the computer you want to go into a 'hi-res' mode, using a special PMODE command. (There are four different hi-res modes, taking up different amounts of memory and offering different resolutions and color choices.) Once you have done this, you need to use hi-res graphics commands like DRAW and MOVE, and you can no longer print characters on the screen. So, to program a game using hi-res graphics,, you might open in text mode, print the instructions, then go into hi-res mode to draw the game board, and then go back into text mode to print the score.

On the Commodore 64, which has twice as much memory, you can use all the available graphics modes at once. A fixed amount of memory is allocated to each 'block' of dots; but you can decide (and tell the computer) what the code stored in each part of that memory will stand for. You might use lots of bits to describe color, and relatively few to fix the display pattern; you might use some of the bits to give a character code; you might settle for a limited color choice, and use most of the bits to fix a complex on/off dot pattern. You could, for example, center a heading at the top of the screen, draw a 'background' using all sixteen available colors at only modest resolution, and then, in the foreground, draw a figure in great detail using only two colors in each screen-memory block. The disadvantage of this system is that the computer doesn't have a range of specialized commands for use in each mode.

On the BBC computers, there are up to seven different modes. Only one can be used at a time, which you have to select (unless you use the default mode in which the machine switches on) by giving a MODE command. Each mode supports both text and graphics, but each offers a different combination of memory space, graphics resolution and color choice. Only one mode provides graphics characters, but user-defined characters are available in all other modes.

The BBC computers offer another facility that can come in very handy: the concept of 'windows'. What is a window? In fact, the word is used in two slightly different ways. It is perhaps easiest to think of a window as being part of the screen, which you set aside for a particular purpose – typically, either for graphics or for

Windows

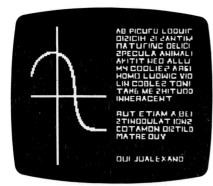

Using windows, different parts of the screen can be allocated for different purposes without, for example, text overrunning onto graphics displays. You might want to show a mathematical or business graph with some commentary alongside or underneath. Windows would come in very useful here. So too would they if you were planning to display a picture with an accompanying caption. Windows can also be used for zeroing in on a particular part of a much larger display held in coded form in the computer's memory. Any part of a 'page' of memory can be accessed in this way, using one or more windows. Another useful facility of windows is that they can move steadily over the page, in a 'scrolling' action, or hop about all over the page, as required. Applied to graphics, this can be used to provide a close-up view of any of the details drawn on the screen. On some computer models, you can make a graphics window with high-resolution mode, using ordinary text mode for everything outside it.

text. You might, for instance, divide the screen into two and tell the computer to use the left-hand side for text and the right-hand side for pictures; or you might, say, draw illustrations on all but the bottom three or four lines and reserve these for captions.

The advantage of defining windows is that the computer will automatically separate the text and the graphics. You don't have to put elaborate instructions into your program to ensure that the caption doesn't run over and obscure part of the graph!

In a slightly different use, you might think of the display that is on screen as just a section of a much larger display that is in the computer's memory. Imagine looking at a drawing 12 inches (30 centimeters) square, through a template with a 4-inch (10-centimeter) square hole cut into it. By moving the template, you can see all of the drawing, but only part of it at any one time.

You may be used to thinking of the computer working this way in connection with word processing (where only a part of a long document is displayed at a time), or spreadsheet analysis (where only a part of a large tabular calculation is displayed at a time). The screen may 'jump' from one view to another, or 'scroll' steadily up, down or across the page.

On some computers that use the window concept, you can set up a memory 'page' holding display data on an area much larger than the screen. You then open one or more windows onto the memory page, using part or all of the screen, to look at parts of it. (You might keep your spreadsheet headings in view through one window, while scrolling down and using another one to look at the bottom lines.) The advantage in graphics programming is that you can use a high 'theoretical' resolution for your graphics to obtain a close-up view of one part after another of your design, graph or drawing.

The disadvantage is that the window concept is not easy for everyone to work with! To get a better grasp of the idea, let's look at another example. The NewBrain is a computer that works entirely in window mode. Its memory 'display editor' can hold a page of up to 255 lines of text. The screen can show a maximum of thirty lines of this, and the display can scroll up and down the page to show different sections of the text. On this page you can set aside a graphics section – rather like drawing a pencil line around a space on a piece of paper and marking 'picture here' – and in that graphics window (part or all of which may appear on the actual screen) you can use the hi-res commands PLOT, TURN, DRAW, and so on. Elsewhere on the page, you carry on using text PRINTing commands in the usual way.

Graphics programs

So far, we've been talking as if the computer holds all the information it needs to draw a display in memory. This is just what it does, when the display is actually on the screen. However, the way that the cathode-ray tube works, which is the basis of the television screen display, means the computer has to keep on redrawing the picture, many times a second, before it fades from view.

When you run a program, though, the display will change many times. The computer will PRINT different messages to you, draw different images on top of those already on screen, or sometimes clear the screen and start again. Does the computer hold all the different screenfuls of information in memory all at once, then?

No, of course it doesn't. That's why you can't 'scroll up' a normal exchange of information with the computer and see what it replied a hundred lines before. Instead, the program itself gives the computer instructions on how to update its display memory as and when it needs to do so. The computer only has one 'page' of screen memory: it keeps 'erasing' and 'writing in' (electronically, that is) information, as the program tells it to.

In this way, you can set up a 'dynamic' display. You can watch the computer 'draw' a line across the screen; you can have the computer draw a rocket and make it 'take off' up the screen, and so on. In effect, you're watching the computer at work as it updates its display register and promptly changes the picture it presents.

This is very handy, because it means that you can produce simple animated effects with a minimum of memory. The disadvantage, however, is that the picture changes only slowly, element by element. The speed may seem fine if you're drawing a very simple cartoon character, using a few short BASIC statements and then redrawing it a fraction further across the screen, but not if you want to change several elements instantaneously of an elaborately programmed display. It can take the computer several seconds, even minutes, to update large chunks of its display register.

The way to get around this problem, and to switch immediately from one picture to another – as a movie switches from one frame to another – is to put several pages of display information into memory. You can then use a single command sequence to tell the computer to switch from displaying one page, to displaying another.

Many computers allow you to do this switching. On the TRS-80 Color Computer, with 32K of RAM, for instance, you can set up as many as eight pages provided that you keep the memory requirement for each page fairly low by limiting the resolution and colour choice. On the Commodore 64, you can choose between four pages for general display information, but there is only one section of the main 'colour memory', which can make life tricky. On the NewBrain, you can set up as many pages as you can support in memory.

Each page of memory, however, occupies a lot of space. Even if details of beautiful graphics displays take up most of your program, you still have to find some room in memory for the instructions and for the computer to use as workspace. Because of this, the animation effects you can achieve with a small home computer are limited. To produce animated videos of professional quality, you need more sophisticated equipment and to pay a professional price!

Sprites

One very handy device which simplifies the programming of moving shapes is the 'sprite'. Let's look briefly at moving shapes, and at the way sprites are used.

How do you normally move an object across the screen, using BASIC statements? You plan out the shape you want to move, which might cover more than one graphics location (character space, pixel or dot), on squared paper. We'll use a simple 'space invader'-type character as our example and draw it over nine locations, using fairly standard graphics characters in each location. (The same principles would apply if you used user-defined characters to get greater definition or drew the shape over many more dot locations.) You then set up one or more variables to hold details on the

Sprites

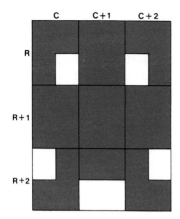

129	128	130
128	128	128
136	131	132

screen location (row and column) at which you want to print the shape. Let's mark our variables, R and C, as on the figure above.

You then set up a sequence of BASIC (or other language) statements (in a subroutine, or procedure, or whatever type of program module your language lets you use) which tell the computer how to draw the shape. Ours might look like this:

```
500   REM SUBROUTINE TO DRAW INVADER
510   PRINT@(R,C), CHR$(129)+CHR$(128)
      +CHR$(130)
520   PRINT@ (R+1,C), CHR$(128)+CHR$(128)
      +CHR$(128)
530   PRINT@ (R+2,C), CHR$(136)+CHR$(131)
      +CHR$(132)
540   RETURN
```

Of course, if you were moving the shape in a regular pattern, you might program in a 'blank border', too, so that it erased itself each time you moved it. We'll skip that refinement for now.

Finally, you set up a section of the program that updates the values of R and C, erases the shape and redraws it at the new screen location, each time you want to move it, like this:

```
10  REM MOVING INVADER
20  FOR X = 1 TO 10
30  READ R,C
40  GOSUB 400: REM ERASES PREVIOUS
    VERSION
50  GOSUB 500: REM DRAWS NEW VERSION
60  NEXT X
70  DATA 5,10,5,11,6,11,6,12,7,12
80  DATA 7,13,7,14,8,14,8,13,8,12
```

Not particularly hard to program, but long-winded. Each time you move the shape, you have to give the computer the complete set of instructions that enable it to erase and redraw. That's around fifteen lines of program for the computer to work through (including the 'erase' subroutine, which we haven't given you) each time it redraws the shape.

Using a sprite, you can cut this down considerably. A sprite is a fairly large shape, covering several locations, which you can define and then move as a whole. The computer has a special set of registers in memory where the details of the sprite's pattern are held. The way it works is rather like making a giant user-defined character. You feed in the exact pattern of blacks and whites (or colors, if your computer lets you) you require, and then the computer stores these under a code-name, Sprite 2, for instance. You then tell the computer where to print Sprite 2, using variables, as we did before. But, instead of going through a subroutine that gives all the details of the character each time you redraw it, you just tell the computer to 'erase Sprite 2', and then 'redraw Sprite 2' (using suitable commands, of course). The result is not only quicker to program: it is also quicker for the computer to execute.

We have used the sprites on the Commodore 64, a computer which doesn't have good hi-res commands. Consequently, you have to POKE all the necessary details into the computer's memory (how this works is explained in Chapter 7). The programs would not be easy to follow or copy for those using other machines, so it is not worth including any. To give you some idea of the power of the idea, the Commodore can hold data on up to eight sprites, each with a definition of 24 × 21. It can fix their speeds and directions, and can automatically double them in size, either horizontally, vertically or both. It also allocates to them fixed 'priorities', so that one sprite can move smoothly in front of another, and has 'collision detection' facilities so that it can tell when the sprites collide (which is very handy in games).

Sprites are also available on the Texas Instruments 99/4A (with Extended BASIC), and on the Atari computers, where they are called player missile graphics. Each of these machines has a different way of developing this powerful idea.

Color handling

On page 31, we gave you a list of eight colors and codes. They are, in fact, the eight colors most commonly used on home computers. At least, the names are the same; the shades they refer to can appear quite different on different computers and displays! They are also the colors used for Teletext in the UK.

As you probably know, red, green and blue are three 'primaries' for light. All other colors can be made by combining light beams of these three types. The color codes we gave are numbered so that the codes given to these three primary light colors are added to make other colors. Cyan, for instance, is a combination of blue and green. The number for cyan, 6 (0110 in binary, as on page 31), is the sum of the numbers for green (decimal 2, binary 0010), and blue (decimal 4; binary 0100). This is the type of code system you will normally encounter, though the BASIC statements used to change foreground and background colors vary greatly from machine to machine.

Most color computers offer a minimum of eight colors, though they don't always include black and white, and not all colors can be used in all modes. Other common colors are buff and orange. Some computers offer nine colors, using black or white separately from the 'main set' of eight. Others claim to offer sixteen. But be warned. Though there are, in fact, sixteen different colors on, for instance, the Commodore 64, there are only eight different ones on the BBC microcomputers, for example, and the other 'colors' that make up the advertised total are flashing on/off combinations of the original color set.

On many computers, it is possible to give the impression of other colors by printing alternate dots of two different colors, in a checkerboard pattern. Alternating red and yellow, for instance, gives the illusion of orange from a short distance. More sophisticated techniques can still further enhance the range. The Atari computers, for example, offer sixteen different brightness levels for each of their sixteen colors. Many games on offer for the Apple II computer make subtle and exciting use of color by 'shading over' the original hues in different ways. To do this, however, you need to be an experienced programmer, and/or have a special graphics program which helps you get the effect.

BASIC graphics commands on one computer

We cannot describe here the full range of graphics commands available even in BASIC, let alone in other graphics-oriented languages like LOGO. To give you an idea of what a fairly good version of BASIC can do to help you with your graphics, let's look at the major commands available in the Microsoft BASIC used on the Dragon 32. As we explained in the Introduction, the same or very similar commands are used on a wide range of other machines. The programs that appear later in the book are all written in Microsoft BASIC, and so this section will also serve as an explanation of any unfamiliar statements you may find there.

At low resolution, this version of BASIC uses PRINT@ as its main 'positioning' tool. The working screen is 16 rows of 32 characters, numbering both rows and columns from 0. A single number can thus be used to describe screen character positions, so the range of permissible numbers is 0 to 511.

There are nine colors available in low resolution. At higher resolutions, only limited combinations of them can be used. It is a fairly standard set, with the following decimal number codes:

Black	0	Green	1
Yellow	2	Blue	3
Red	4	Buff	5
Cyan	6	Magenta	7
Orange	8		

(No white, as you see.) Background colors are selected using CLS. For instance, CLS 6 turns the screen cyan.

A maddening feature of Dragon BASIC is that it is normally only practicable to use text in black on a green background. Our programs try to show how this can be turned into a positive feature (see the display for Dice on page 107, for instance). There are sixteen graphics characters which can be accessed only through CHR$ statements. The foreground color for these is always black; the background color can be changed by altering the code number. For instance, CHR$(140) produces a black and green shape; CHR$(204) the same shape, but with a buff background. It is not possible to define additional characters.

As we said earlier, medium resolution and low resolution can be used together. The medium-resolution screen is 64 × 32 pixels, and this time two numbers (first column, then row) are used to locate each pixel. The command SET (followed by column, row and color numbers) is used to turn pixels on. RESET turns them off again. POINT can be used to find out if any pixel is on or off; you will find this used in some of our games.

Hi-res graphics have to be used entirely separately from low and medium resolution. You will find them in, for instance, Artist on page 114. There are five different modes, as follows:

0 128 × 96, two-color (choice of two color sets)
1 128 × 96, four-color (again, from two sets: uses more memory)
2 192 × 128, two-color
3 198 × 128, four-color
4 256 × 192, two-color

The two-color sets are black/green (0) or black/buff (1). The four-color sets are buff/cyan/magenta/orange (1), or green/yellow/blue/red (0). There is no way of changing the colors in each set.

These are the 'utility' commands which set up the appropriate mode:

PMODE: followed by a number indicating the hi-res mode, and another designating a graphics memory page to be used.

SCREEN: followed by a number indicating the type (0 for text; 1 for hi-res) and another the color set.

COLOR followed by codes for foreground and back-

Hi-res graphics

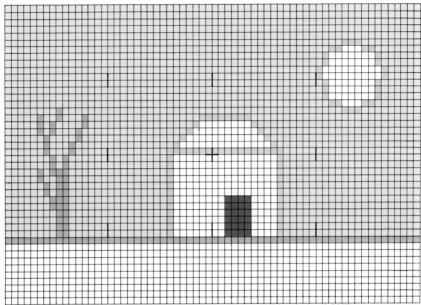

Let's illustrate typical hi-res commands by drawing a simple picture on a 'mini-screen':
First we'll choose a suitable four-color mode and clear the screen:

```
10    PMODE 1,1: SCREEN 1,0
20    PCLS
```

We'll have a blue background and green foreground for this picture:

```
30    COLOR 1,3
```

Now let's use LINE commands to draw the ground and PAINT it:

```
40    LINE (0,9) – (63,9), PSET
50    PAINT (0,0), 1, 1
```

to draw the tree:

```
60    LINE (8,19) – (9,10), PSET, BF
70    LINE (5,19) – (7,14), PSET
```

```
80    LINE (5,27) – (7,19), PSET
90    LINE (8,28) – (7,25), PSET
100   LINE (12,27) – (9,20), PSET
```

(notice the computer 'approximates' straight lines) and to draw the door:

```
110   LINE (34,15) – (37,10), PSET, BF
```

We'll use a CIRCLE command to draw a yellow sun, and then PAINT it:

```
120   CIRCLE (53,33), 5,2: PAINT (53,33), 2, 2
```

And finally we'll use relative DRAW commands to sketch the outline of the house:

```
130   DRAW C4; BM 25, 10; U12; E5, R7; G5; NL
      16; D12
```

(notice the color, 'blank move' to start, and 'no update' codes included in the DRAW statement).

ground colors.

PCLS, PSET, PRESET, PPOINT: the hi-res equivalents of CLS, SET, RESET and POINT.

And these are the special hi-res graphics commands:

LINE: draws lines from one pair of absolute coordinates to another. In other words, two coordinates from the hi-res screen map are given to locate each end of the line. (If only one pair is given, the current cursor position is used as the starting point.) LINE is also followed by PSET or PRESET to draw the line in foreground or background color respectively. Following this by B draws a rectangle using the points given to locate the diagonal corners. BF fills the rectangle with the foreground color.

DRAW: draws lines in relative mode. In other words, there is no need to give screen coordinates, just instructions like 'up 10' or 'down 15'. These are the character codes which follow it:

U, D, L and R: up, down, left and right

E, F, G and N: at 45, 135, 225, and 315 degrees from vertical

C: change color

A: displace by angle given (1, 2, 3 or 4=0, 90, 180, 270 degrees)

S: change scale of drawing. 1 is quarter scale, 4 existing scale. Maximum 62.

N: leave starting position unchanged.

M: move to coordinates given, or by amounts given (+ or −).

BM: blank move (change starting point, do not draw).

PAINT: starts painting from coordinates given and paints in color given until painting reaches a border of another color given; e.g. PAINT (10,10), 4, 6 fills the screen with red, starting at location 10,10, until a cyan border is reached.

CIRCLE: followed by a center coordinate, radius, color, and possibly other codes to indicate an arc or ellipse.

GET and PUT: a pair of commands which imitate in some ways a sprite capability. By GETting a section of the screen display (a rectangle of any size, with coordinates you give), you tell the computer to store it in an array which you set up. You can then PUT it back elsewhere on the screen. A very handy way of drawing a row or random pattern of identical elements.

Dragon BASIC is not the most flexible form of BASIC available, but it is easy to work with, and can generate a wide variety of different displays, as you will see from our programs.

4 Sounds from your computer

Sounds are particularly interesting to games players, because a very simple range of sound effects can really bring a computer game to life. Interestingly, penny arcades have found that when an arcade game loses its sound, players will not touch it, even if the rest of its circuitry is working perfectly! It seems that we like the sound feedback to tell us what's going on.

That is not only true in games, of course. Many computers use their sound facilities to produce a simple 'beep' whenever a key is pressed, for instance. Very simple sounds are easy to generate on any home computer that has sound capability, as we shall see. Some computers have far more complex abilities, and can be programmed much like a specialist music synthesizer. However, you need musical knowledge to program these, just as you do to play any musical instrument. In this chapter, we will be concentrating on simple effects you can achieve with minimal musical knowledge.

How computers make sounds

As well as representing numbers, letters or graphical information, the binary code with which the computer works can, indirectly, represent sound wave patterns. To the computer, this code is, of course, an electronic signal, called a digital signal. Electronically, the binary digits are represented by two different voltages (usually 5 volts or thereabouts for binary 1, and 0 volts, or a very low voltage, for binary 0). To show the signal changes or pulses, as they are known, graphically, we use a special kind of wave, known as a 'square wave', that can take only one of, two values at any point. The two values, 1 and 0, are the 'top' and 'bottom' of the wave, as is shown in the diagram. The computer can send sequences of bits (binary digits) to the circuitry that controls its loudspeaker, and depending upon the time interval between which the 1 signal changes to a 0 (the pulse 'width'), and vice versa, so the frequency of the sound wave (the undulations in, say, a second) will vary.

Square waves

The square wave represents the voltage changes of the computer's digital signal, plotted against time. Notice that, theoretically, the change from high voltage to low (from 1 to 0), or vice versa, is instantaneous. This is because the computer's electronic signal allows only one of two possible states at any time, with nothing in between. (The same, of course, applies to the binary code.) The greater the number of fluctuations (pulses) within a given time span, the higher the frequency of the wave.

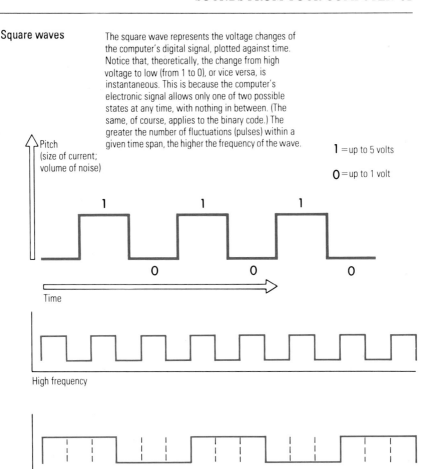

1 = up to 5 volts

0 = up to 1 volt

Pitch
(size of current;
volume of noise)

Time

High frequency

Low frequency

Take a look at the square waves in our illustration. In the top diagram, the signal changes from 1 to 0 and back again very rapidly. This square wave itself thus has a very high frequency. In the bottom diagram the square wave is of a lower frequency because the signal changes much less often. The electrical pulses that the computer generates are transformed by a loudspeaker into sound waves, either of a high frequency (a high-pitched note), if the original digital signal changed rapidly, or, if a series of longer pulses, a low-frequency sound wave (a low-pitched note).

A very simple computer sound generator works in this way. It sends patterns of electrical pulses to its built-in loudspeaker, or to an external loudspeaker to which it may be connected (frequently the one on your TV set). We then hear them as simple 'notes' or 'beeps'. As they are not particularly musical, 'beep' is perhaps a better description.

Let's look briefly at the Timex 2000/Spectrum to see how a very simple sound capability works. The BEEP command produces notes of a duration and pitch which the programmer chooses. The duration is given in seconds, though you can specify part of a second if you wish. The pitch is described as a number. Middle C is 0, and the semitones are numbered at intervals of one up or down from that. So twelve whole numbers represent all the notes in one musical octave. If you want to adjust the tuning, you must specify the pitch more precisely. A statement like

BEEP 1,2

using two parameters, would make the computer play the D above middle C (C=0; C ♯ = 1; D = 2) for one second; and

BEEP .75,0.01

would play a note very marginally above middle C for three-quarters of a second.

By building up a sequence of BEEP commands, and PAUSEs between where you need them, you can make the computer play a very simple tune. You would have to be a pretty desperate musician to use the Spectrum for serious music-making, but the sound it makes is fine for enlivening games. These are the sort of uses to which

Musical notation

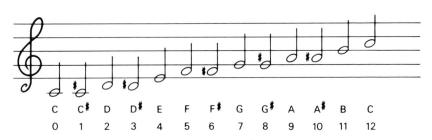

C	C♯	D	D♯	E	F	F♯	G	G♯	A	A♯	B	C
0	1	2	3	4	5	6	7	8	9	10	11	12

the sound capability might be put:

A high BEEP when you hit a target, and perhaps a low BEEP when you miss.

A BEEP to tell you when the computer has worked out its move at chess. (This could take several minutes, so you might need a reminder to get back to the screen.)

A short tune to introduce a new phase in a game, or as a reward for the player who wins.

One point to bear in mind is that, with simple commands like this, some computers – though not all – stick at the BEEP statement until it has finished making the sound. So a one-second BEEP is equivalent to a one-second delay in the program. Sometimes, of course, this is handy; sometimes it can be a problem, and you may find that you have to limit the sound effects in your games to avoid slowing them down too much.

Writing music programs using BEEP is quite a long, slow job, because you have to put in a separate BEEP command before each note, and a PAUSE command for each pause. An example of a slightly more sophisticated command is PLAY on the Dragon and Tandy/Radio Shack machines. PLAY can be followed by a string of data, not just by two parameters. You can include variables, and even variable strings (whole musical phrases), in the string. You can include PAUSE instructions, rather than using a separate program statement for PAUSE. And you can set the volume, by giving a number from 1 to 31.

Some simple sound commands produce sounds that do not exactly correspond to musical notes because the computer is always slightly out of tune. More elaborate commands like PLAY are properly tuned, and to emphasize the point you can replace the numbers that describe the pitch, by the letters A to G, plus ♯ and – symbols to indicate sharps and flats. Another parameter tells the computer which octave (there are five to choose from) to use. Here's a typical PLAY statement:

PLAY O1L4GGP4L3FF

This is telling the computer to play notes in Octave 1 (O1); first with a length of 4 (the exact duration of this depends upon the tempo, which you can also alter), and then later with a length of 3. Two Gs are played, followed by a pause, then two Fs.

You can see the Dragon's PLAY command at work in our 'Organ Player' program on page 92. This simple program lets you play tunes in 'real time', using the keyboard as you would an organ keyboard. If you have a different computer, you may be able to adapt the program or, alternatively, you may find a similar program for your machine in a book or magazine.

Making more complex music

Though the sound generated by a regular-frequency square wave sound is quite pleasant to listen to, it is very limited. Traditional musical instruments produce sounds with much more elaborate wave patterns and notes that vary throughout their duration in volume and sometimes in pitch, too. A computer that aspires to imitate them needs to have a way of 'shaping' notes, and ideally a way of generating different waveforms too.

The ENVELOPE function does the first of these. You follow it by a series of different numbers (14, on the BBC machine) which describe the note in detail, dividing it into four phases: ATTACK, DECAY, SUSTAIN and RELEASE. By altering the values for pitch and volume in these phases, it's possible to produce a fair imitation of, for instance, a flute or a drum, as well as sound effects such as foghorns, thunder claps and rumbling noises.

Using different waveforms with envelope shaping is possible on the Commodore 64. This machine can produce three different waveform shapes: the standard square wave, a sawtooth wave and a triangle wave. Notes made up of these can then be shaped with a volume ADSR envelope.

Computers with ENVELOPE capability generally also provide several different sound channels. You can program these to play different notes simultaneously, and thus have the computer play a tune in harmony – a much richer effect than you can get using a single note at a time. The BBC computer and the Commodore 64 both provide three different music channels. Of course, the computer has to go on, after encountering the first SOUND command (used with ENVELOPE to produce a sound), to see if there are any more to be played with it. That means that it doesn't 'stop work' when it's playing a note. Special circuitry keeps the note going while the computer works on down the program.

Waveforms and envelopes

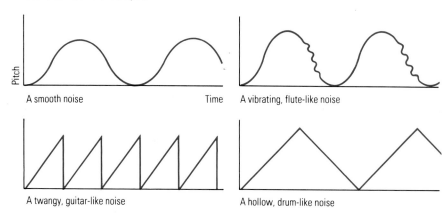

A smooth noise   Time   A vibrating, flute-like noise

A twangy, guitar-like noise   A hollow, drum-like noise

The sounds made by different musical instruments produce different waveforms, as is shown above. This is one of the reasons why, say, a flute and a guitar do not sound the same, even though they may be playing notes of the same pitch. When the string on an instrument is plucked, or a key is struck, the volume of the sound produced changes several times and then dies away. This pattern, known as an envelope, is commonly divided into four phases: attack, decay, sustain and release (ADSR). Computers with a musical capability can approximate the envelopes of different musical instruments. A typical example – the computer envelope of a piano – is shown below. The shaded area indicates the rise and fall of the pitch. Using the computer's ENVELOPE function, and other commands to vary the values of pitch and volume within the four phases, it is often possible to imitate different musical instruments as well as a variety of other sound effects.

Envelopes

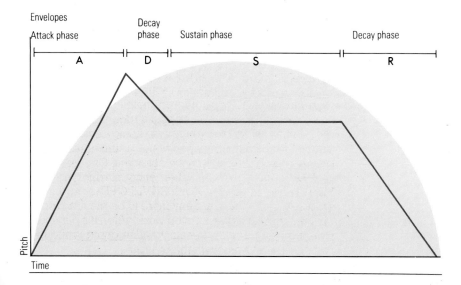

White noise

We need to mention one special type of 'noise'–as opposed to sound–'white' noise. This is the kind of formless noise you hear from, for instance, a radio that is not tuned to a station. It has an irregular waveform.

The computer can produce white noise just as it produces random numbers, by relying upon the complexity of its circuitry to generate a random bit sequence. Many computers can do this as well as, or instead of, producing more or less musical notes. The BBC microcomputer, for instance, has three 'music' sound channels and one noise channel. This can produce eight different types of noise (with different waveforms, at different frequencies, and either separately generated or linked to the frequency of another sound channel).

It is white noise that gives rise to loudspeaker hiss or television screen 'snow'. Its characteristic waveform is shown here.

White noises are particularly handy in games. They are used to produce crashes, bangs, explosions, and so on. If your computer has this capability, you will find plenty of examples of its use in space games.

Playing 'real' music with your programs

Though it may be fun to experiment with your computer's sound commands, there are other ways in which you can generate sound to accompany your programs. Don't forget your trusty tape recorder! You can use its capabilities to enliven your programs with sound, or noise, even if your computer has no built-in sound facilities. You can simply use normal audio recordings with your computer programs – even recording them on the same tapes as your programs if you wish (but on a different section of the tape, of course). Then you can play the tape to produce a 'soundtrack' of music or commentary to go with the display on the video screen.

This works especially well if your computer has a 'remote' control, enabling it to switch the cassette recorder on and off for itself. Then you can put a MOTOR ON or MOTOR OFF command (the exact words used vary from system to system) into your program and synchronize the sound and pictures. You could even vary the pace, by including an INPUT or INKEY$ statement, and only switching the motor on when the user presses a key. Here's an example:

```
50   A$ = INKEY$
60   IF A$ = "Y" THEN MOTOR ON ELSE GOTO 50
70   (next section of program, with soundtrack)
```

A computer system for sound

A convenient way to produce sound to go with your programs – and one that is easily overlooked – is to use your cassette recorder. In fact, if your computer does not have sound capabilities, this is about the only way it can be done. You can use the same tape for recording both the program and the soundtrack accompaniment.

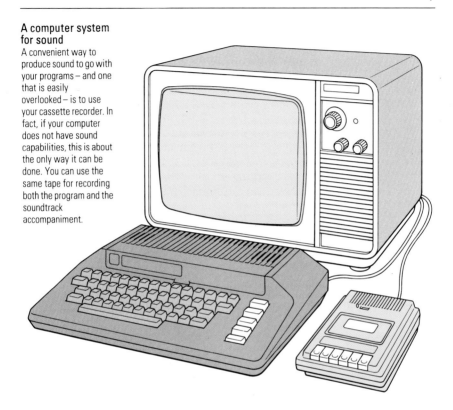

To get the sound properly synchronized, leave some spaces in between your comments on the tape!

One machine with the particular capability we have been describing is the TRS-80 Color Computer. You plug in the 'remote' lead, press PLAY on your tape recorder, and leave it to the computer to get the recorder going and to stop it, as necessary. There is also another command, AUDIO ON/OFF, which is additional to MOTOR ON/OFF. This directs the sound from the tape recorder into the television loudspeaker. Of course, on many machines it won't play over the cassette recorder's own loudspeaker if you've connected the earphone socket to the computer! By juggling with the AUDIO command, you can make sure that users hear the music or messages to go with your program, without hearing the program listing itself, at top volume.

Speech synthesis

Using cassette control commands (if your computer has them), you can have your own voice, or any other sounds you care to record on tape, accompany your program. But what about having the computer 'speak' to you?

Speech synthesis is quite well established, and there are several systems that make home computers 'speak'. The more effective ones use a special hardware device, called a speech synthesizer chip. The circuitry on this contains the data the computer needs to produce the waveforms that make up a small vocabulary. When you tell the computer to 'speak' words, the correct waveforms are generated, and something resembling speech emerges.

Speech synthesizer chips are becoming quite common. The Texas Instruments TI99/4A has such a speech synthesis peripheral, and there are several available for Sinclair/Timex computers. We have a Torch computer with a speech synthesis chip inside it, and so get spoken sound effects accompanying a 'snake' game, for instance. Whenever the snake 'eats' a number, a voice tells us how many we have scored. 'Out', it intones when we make a mistake and lose the game.

It is possible to produce a roughly similar effect using software alone. In that case, the computer's normal processing facilities are pressed into service to produce speech 'envelopes'. To take one example, there is a program available on cassette for the Timex 2000/ Sinclair Spectrum that claims to let you say aloud a phrase of your choice, which the computer will then codify and reproduce. Doing it this way, you can choose your own vocabulary, instead of being confined to the pretty limited vocabularies of the synthesizer chips.

One thing to bear in mind when investing in this kind of additional capability (and the same applies to devices like joysticks and light pens, which we talk about in the next chapter) is that not many commercially produced programs will make use of them. By no means all users of your computer will have opted to buy such extras, and software manufacturers try to cater for as large a market as possible. The devices will only come into their own if you are prepared to write programs using them.

5 Computer hardware

In this chapter, we will take a look at the hardware of computer systems, from the point of view of the games player. What kind of systems can be used for games and graphics? What features should you look out for? What equipment can you add to your system to make it more fun to use?

The basic computer
You can play games on just about any computer, though some are more obviously designed for the purpose than others. Some have color and sound, for instance, while others concentrate more on powerful arithmetical abilities. What are the general features that make one computer a better tool for playing games than another?

Computer memory
Without a doubt, the most important feature is the size of your computer's memory. That determines how complicated the programs can be that are run on it. To store programs takes up part of the memory, and more memory is needed for workspace – to hold variable information, data for screen displays, and so on. If your computer has a small memory, it will only handle small programs.

If you have a computer with less than, say, 5K (that is, just over 5000 bytes) of random access memory (RAM), then you will find that its uses are very restricted. It will only be able to handle simple games programs: race games, games like 'Breakout', simple guessing games, and so on. Commercial programmers have used a lot of ingenuity in developing good games programs for small machines, but the results do not compare in terms of sophistication with a program that runs on a larger computer (that is, a computer with a larger memory). You won't find any small-machine versions of memory-hungry games, and you won't find any games using high-resolution graphics. (Such games for these machines can be obtained in cartridge form, though.)

Many middle-range home computers have 16K of RAM. Bigger ones may have 32, 48 or 64K. Some machines are offered in several different versions: one with a modest-sized RAM, and one with a larger one. Is it worth paying the extra – and it can be a lot – for the additional memory? Yes, if you want to do anything remotely ambitious with your computer.

Look in a local store, or computer magazine, for instance, at the range of games available for the Timex 2000/Sinclair Spectrum, a very popular computer which comes with either 16K or 48K of RAM. There are some very good games for the smaller machine (which will, of course, also run on the larger one). They include arcade games such as Hungry Horace, Meteor Storm and Specters, shortish adventure games like Sorcerer's Castle and Faust Folly, and simpler simulations such as Nightflight (less dramatic than day flight – you don't get much of a display of the ground!). But only for the 48K version can you get graphic adventures like The Hobbit and Pimania, good chess programs, higher-quality arcade games like Penetrator, and so on. As we saw in Chapter 3, high-resolution graphics takes up an enormous amount of memory space, and you will find more ambitious graphics displays in the programs written for the more powerful home computers.

It is also worth considering, as well as the quality of bought programs, the quality of programs you will be writing for yourself. A 16K memory will suffice to write a pretty good game – by our definition, one that you can keep on playing for longer than it took you to type it into the computer! It will do fine, for instance, for the kind of programs included later in this book. But, to do anything really ambitious, 16K is simply not enough for the non-expert programmer writing in BASIC (which eats up far more memory than the machine code in which many commercial games are written) to do anything really ambitious. If you have less than 16K, you will find the 'Out of Memory' message coming up pretty frequently, and you will possibly spend more time cutting down on memory requirements than in planning the 'play' aspects of your program.

Graphics and sound facilities

What about other aspects of your computer? Graphics and sound facilities are obviously very important to you. Here you may want to distinguish between two aspects:

what the machine itself can do, and what you can do with the machine.

Let us look first at what the machine can do. Even simple machines can be persuaded to generate very attractive screen displays using low-resolution graphics. If your computer includes the ability to user-define characters, this adds a very powerful tool to its low-resolution capabilities. A display with, say, a user-defined man and his dog tramping around a field rounding up user-defined sheep can be very impressive. Without the user-definition, you have to resort to text and graphics characters. Steering a little asterisk across the screen is not as much fun as steering a recognizable spaceship, though the game will otherwise be played in just the same way.

High resolution is perhaps overrated. It comes into its own when the computer 'draws' elaborate pictures like the one we sketched out on page 48; and it certainly scores for graph-making and other business or scientific uses. But, in most machines, you only have a limited range of colors in high resolution – generally only two in the very highest resolution available. Many games look better in a range of colors at a lower resolution. That is if your computer has color, of course. If it doesn't – as with the Timex 1000/Sinclair ZX81, for example – you really are missing something (though doubtless saving some money).

What about sound? A 'noise' channel is useful for games, though not all computers offer one. A single sound channel is okay for limited sound effects, but really no good for playing music. Three or four channels, with 'envelope' facilities, are wonderful. However, it is not easy for you, or for many commercial programmers for that matter, to make full use of elaborate sound facilities. You will find that the extra quality of the sound in machines such as the BBC microcomputer or the Commodore 64 often does not mean better-quality games. Perhaps more important is the computer's ability to amplify sound: passing it through an external amplifier instead of a tiny built-in loudspeaker. Most built-in loudspeakers will not produce deafening explosions when the spaceship blows up – more like a muffled or very subdued 'pffutt'.

Let us return now to the question of what you can do with your computer's abilities. In some machines, the enhanced hardware features (e.g., high-resolution graphics and sound) are not fully supported by the BASIC, and to use them in your programs you have to write in machine code or simulate machine code in BASIC by using PEEK and POKE commands (we consider these in Chapter 7). In other machines, the BASIC (or other high-level language, such as FORTH) does cover all the major features – though a dedicated machine-code programmer will generally be able to extract that much more performance than a BASIC programmer. If, of course, you plan to buy most of your programs prewritten, this won't matter too much to you.

The better games programs, written by experts for machines like the Commodore VIC-20 and 64, and the Atari 400 and 800, use their features to the limit. They score over most of those games programs written for machines that offer less exciting capabilities (in relation to their price) such as the TRS-80 Color Computer and the Timex 2000/Sinclair Spectrum. If, however, you plan to write programs yourself, you may really curse the lack of good graphics and sound commands on the Commodore and Atari machines. On the Timex 2000/Spectrum, for example, you can write an enjoyable game without too much effort, while on the Commodore 64, writing the same game in BASIC could take five times as long. You could write a better game for the Commodore, making full use of its flexible graphics and three-channel sound, but that might take even twenty times as long. Is it worth spending so much more time? Only you can decide.

Expanding your machine

When choosing a computer you should consider not only the machine's built-in facilities you need now, but also any extra equipment you may want to use with it in the future. This is an important issue, and one that is not always put across in the advertisements.

How can you add on hardware to your computer? Basically there are two ways. First, you can open the computer case and slot in extra components – normally chips or cards, which fit slots left vacant for them on the computer's circuit board. (This is a job for the moder-

Ports and connectors

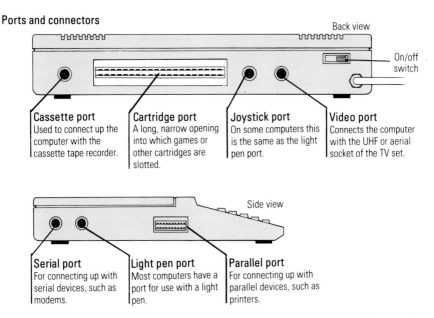

Back view

On/off switch

Cassette port
Used to connect up the computer with the cassette tape recorder.

Cartridge port
A long, narrow opening into which games or other cartridges are slotted.

Joystick port
On some computers this is the same as the light pen port.

Video port
Connects the computer with the UHF or aerial socket of the TV set.

Side view

Serial port
For connecting up with serial devices, such as modems.

Light pen port
Most computers have a port for use with a light pen.

Parallel port
For connecting up with parallel devices, such as printers.

ately expert: ask your computer dealer to do it for you.) Second, you can connect equipment to your computer by using its own external connectors. These may be in the form of sockets, into which you plug leads – virtually all home computers have cassette player sockets, for instance – or they may be in the form of 'edge connectors'. A hole in the casing literally exposes an edge of the circuit board, and the equipment is connected directly to this. A special variation on the edge connector is the cartridge slot, into which you can slip a cartridge containing circuitry which then connects directly to the circuit board.

There are different types of port – 'port' is the general word for connection point. These differences are not only physical, they also include software differences – the different ways ports are programmed to communicate with various types of equipment. We cannot discuss the types in detail here. The important thing is to discover what type of connection ports your computer offers, and what type of port is required by the equipment you plan to use with it.

Sometimes it is possible to provide additional ports

by expanding the existing connection points. You may have seen advertised for popular computers that are quite difficult to expand, like the Timex 1000, units which perform the software and hardware tasks of converting a simple edge connector into a range of ports.

Adding memory One very important way in which you can expand your machine is to make up for the fundamental limitations we have already discussed. If your machine has a small RAM, for instance, you may be able to add extra RAM to it. If it has a limited BASIC, you may be able to add extra BASIC capabilities. If it lacks sound or high-resolution graphics, you may be able to add these facilities.

Let's consider these points in turn. The maximum amount of RAM that a home computer can normally handle at a time is 64K. This is because the computer's microprocessor can only deal with 65,536 addresses at once. To add extra RAM, if yours has less than this, you generally buy either a RAM chip which you fix inside the computer, or a RAM pack, which sits outside it. The former is neater, but not all computers can be fitted with extra RAM chips. RAM packs, on the other hand, can cause trouble if they are not firmly connected. What you can have depends on what is available for your particular machine. All RAM is pretty much the same in use, so it is worth shopping around to locate the size and type you need at the lowest price going.

To make better use of the computer's existing abilities, or of the memory you have added on, you need better commands. This is where Extended BASICs, graphics packs and the like come in. They equip the computer to understand additional high-level commands, and so make it easier to program.

This equipment is easiest to use if it comes in ROM (read only memory) form. You might have a ROM chip or a ROM cartridge, or a completely separate unit, which you link to your computer. Sometimes the commands come in the form of software: coded instructions on cassette, or on a floppy disk. But cassettes, in particular, are a great deal more trouble to handle than ROM devices. Instead of just plugging in the ROM and forgetting about it, you have to LOAD the extra software each time you switch the computer on.

Joysticks and Paddles

Joystick

Paddle

You are possibly familiar with joysticks already. If you have ever played a television game then you will very likely have used them. They are player control devices, with a little 'stick' which you can move around to control one or more symbols on the screen – the cursor, or a spaceship, or a character negotiating a maze, say. They usually have a 'fire' button, too, which you press to fire your missiles, and sometimes additional controls which let you slow down, speed up, or give other orders to the computer.

Most game-oriented home computers (like the Atari computers and the Commodore VIC-20 and 64, for instance) have ports for connecting joysticks. But, of course, joysticks can only be used with programs that have been written to read in data from them. In fact, there are quite a few commercially written programs available for use with joysticks. (It will normally tell you on the pack whether or not joysticks can be used.) You can also write your own programs to use joysticks. We will see how this is done for the Dragon in the 'Breakout' program on page 125.

Lots of different joysticks are available, but not all of them work with all computers, so you should check carefully before choosing them. The more expensive joysticks are often worth the extra, since they tend to be more sensitive and easier to use.

Some computers will not directly support joysticks. The Sinclair/Timex machines won't, for instance. If your computer cannot easily have joysticks, or if you do not wish to pay the extra for them, then you can control your games from the keyboard, using different keys to indicate up, down, right, left, and sometimes other directions, too. Some people find this perfectly all right: others find it difficult, and feel that joysticks are virtually a must. If, however, you take the trouble to connect joysticks to a machine which does not offer them (to do this you will need a device called an interface) you may have difficulty in finding software with which you can use them. (An independent supplier may well have produced what you need.)

Games paddles are similar to joysticks in that they too are used in game control. Some machines offer these as an alternative; many do not.

Timex 2000/ZX Spectrum keyboard

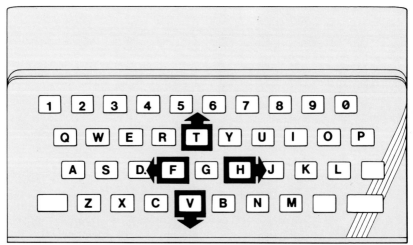

Games displays can be controlled from the keyboard. Sometimes the cursor control keys are used, with or without the shift key (depending on the computer model). On other machines, the central set of keys is used, as on the Timex 2000/Spectrum shown here: the directional arrows are drawn in on keys used in a typical game display. With some games on this machine, up and down movement may be controlled by your left hand using the Z and the Q keys, and left and right by the O and P keys, worked by your right hand. Many games written for home computers ask you at the start of the game to choose which keys you prefer to use.

Light pens   These are fat ball-point-penlike objects. You may have seen them in supermarkets, where they are often used for 'reading' bar-coded information into electronic cash registers. As well as 'reading-in' this type of data, they can be used with the video screen: to point to an item in a list of choices (called a 'menu') or to draw a picture on the screen. The computer can sense where the light pen tip is on the screen, as its circuitry 'scans' the screen to rewrite the display.

Quite a few computers offer light pens as accessories, but, so far, relatively few commercial programs have made use of them. This being so, it might be advisable to wait until you find a suitable program before investing in the pen!

Robots and turtles   Robots aren't used *in* games: using them *is* a game! Some robots, and similar small devices, can be control-led by home computers. This is a field that is likely to

Using a light pen

The light pen works by recognizing the bright spot of light that continuously scans the television screen from side to side and top to bottom. (It is this scanning signal that creates the picture.) As soon as the spot passes beneath the tip of the pen, the computer 'knows', and can calculate, the exact position of the pen in relation to the scanning signal's movement on an invisible screen grid. Many light pens allow a character to be displayed beneath the tip. When this is a dot, the dots can be joined up to form a line, and thus to draw directly on to the screen.

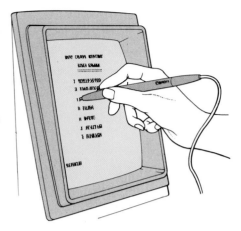

expand over the next few years. All such devices are tied in with software packages, so make sure that your computer can be programmed to control them.

One very special type of robot is the 'turtle'. This is a little dome-shaped device with wheels, which has a pen sunk into its underside. By giving it signals from a computer, you can make it travel in different directions, and lower or raise the pen to draw lines as it goes. 'Turtle graphics' is the name given to this process: often it is done using the LOGO language. If you don't have a mechanical turtle, you can use similar graphics commands to control a visual 'turtle' – a little arrow-shaped mark on your video screen.

The essential thing about turtle graphics is that the turtle is always pointing in a particular direction. Normal graphics commands just describe a point on the screen, and tell the computer to draw from it in a specific direction – up, down, to another point. Turtle graphics commands are more along the lines of 'Go straight on for ten units; then turn left eighty degrees; then go straight for twenty units; then turn round and go back five units'. They can be confusing at first, but many people find them easier to work with than conventional commands.

Other accessories We have not yet mentioned one of the most important accessories of all – a printer! We don't have the space to discuss printers in detail here, but if you are interested

LOGO turtle

The turtle is a kind of robot that can be instructed to draw lines or shapes on paper. Graphics commands to the turtle are normally given in the LOGO language. To tell the turtle how to move, you don't just use fixed coordinates – as is normally done in graphics – but instead relate everything to the turtle's position.

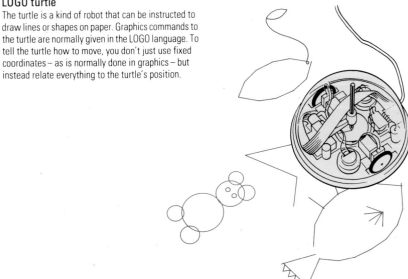

in graphics, you will need to take that into consideration when choosing a printer. Dot matrix printers can often be programmed to print charts, graphs and pictures. It is not so easy to do this with daisy-wheel printers.

Pen plotters are designed specifically for producing graphics. They give a smoother image than any printer, and many of them can work in several colors, using a set of pens at a time. However, they tend to be very expensive for the computer hobbyist.

If you want to do serious work with high-resolution graphics, you may find that the poor display quality of your television is a handicap. A color monitor provides a much better display. There are two main types of monitor, RGB (red-green-blue) and PAL, which both use different signal-generating systems. You can, however, only run a monitor if your computer has a video socket, as opposed to the standard UHF television socket. Sometimes display quality is, in any case, limited by the cheap circuitry inside the computer itself and using a monitor does not improve matters. That is one reason why the very cheapest computers often do not have video sockets.

Pen plotter

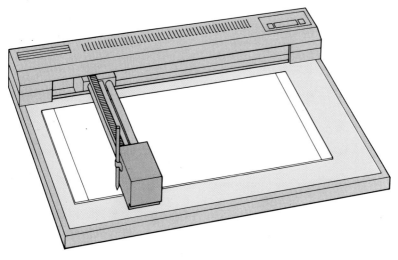

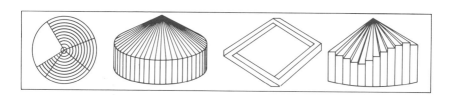

A computer can be programmed to produce high-quality color graphics on paper, using a flat-bed pen plotter (top). On most inexpensive plotters, the pen (or pens) is attached to a bar that moves across the paper; the pen moves up and down, tapping away on the paper as it goes. On some, the paper moves too. Some very simple examples of the kind of graphics that a pen plotter can produce are shown above.

Into the future   The quality of home computers, and the range of equipment available to use with them, improves every day. But what of the future? What can the game-player expect in, say, ten years' time?

One feature that may become more common is a multi-user ability – games played by not just two players, but four or more, each with a separate joystick/controller. With more than two players, of course, it becomes difficult for each one to get an adequate look at the display. However, a second display (and some up-market home computers can support one) will soon solve that problem!

We can expect that really high-quality graphics will become more and more common. Computer memory is becoming cheaper, and this will make it easier for machines to offer high-resolution graphics using lots of colors at the same time. New types of computer display (perhaps using flat screens) could improve the quality and improve the resolution still further.

A lot of the difficulty with graphics, however, lies not in the machine's capabilities but in the time it takes to design screen displays. Improved software should help to cure this problem. Using a light pen, say, it is possible to draw a detailed picture much more rapidly than you could using BASIC commands like DRAW and LINE. Special hardware and software graphics packages will soon make it possible for all of us to produce artistic masterpieces on the small screen!

Already, there is a trend toward more attractive pictures in adventure games, for instance, and in future more and more games should boast really good screen displays. The settings and characters will be more realistic, and the player will be able to control more and more elements. Games based on real-life activities will allow for just about all the factors that influence the real events, not just a few of them.

Cassettes are very awkward to use, as you will know if you have tried! It's easy to spend more time trying to LOAD a game successfully than you spend playing it. Easier-to-use devices such as tape loops and floppy disk drives have become more and more common – and cheaper. As people find more 'serious' uses for their home computers, so they will be able to justify the greater cost of such devices, and make use of them when they play games too.

Whatever equipment you have now, or are just about to buy, you can be pretty certain it will become cheaper over the next few years. But don't wait to take the plunge. Virtually everybody can afford a simple computer system today. By the time you tire of it, you will be able to get a better one at little extra cost. And from there, you can move on to even better things.

6 Writing games programs

In this chapter and the next, we will be looking at games programs you can write for yourself, using BASIC as your programming language. First, we'll discuss how you set about writing games programs: what sort of games you can program for yourself, and how you plan the programs. Then, in Chapter 7, we will talk in more detail about some actual games to program, and give sample listings to show you how they work.

Learning to program

Do you already know something about programming? If not, you will need to learn the rudiments first, either from your computer manual or from a simple book on programming. If you want to concentrate on games and graphics, try to get a book that contains this type of example. Certain programming manuals, you will find, lean heavily on business programs and maths routines.

Some games programs are very simple. Examples like 'guess what number the computer has chosen' appear in many programming books, and as you work through them, you will begin to see how random numbers and other features of BASIC are used in games.

Once you have picked up a little BASIC, a good way to continue is by obtaining program listings for your computer – i.e., lists of program statements for you to type in. You will find many listings in computer magazines. Have a look through several issues to see whether they contain any listings for your machine. (We talk about this in more depth on page 139.) You may also find whole books of programs for your computer. Type in all the programs you can find: it may seem like hours of boring work, but you will begin to see just how the games are written – and to build up a library of simple programs you can use.

You will, of course, also want to buy some programs on cassettes, cartridges or disks. But don't expect to learn too much from them. Often, programs on cassette cannot be listed: they are protected by their writers, so that users will not be able to 'pirate' them. You certainly will not be able to list programs on cartridges. Moreover, though these programs may show you just what your computer can do, they may also set you on the wrong track when you come to write your own programs. The things professional programmers do best – fast action arcade games and the like – are not the best things for you to imitate. Until you are expert, don't try to replace bought programs, just supplement them!

What sort of programs should you write?

When you are only starting, you should not be too ambitious. Forget about selling your first masterpiece to a magazine; instead, concentrate on a few simple programs you will enjoy playing with. You will probably find that you get a great deal more pleasure out of half a dozen simple programs than out of one complicated one. You are also likely to waste less time that way. It can be very disappointing to spend hours and hours on a really ambitious program, only to find that you can't make it work as you had hoped, or – perhaps worse – that you simply don't enjoy playing the game.

Many of the old games are very good. You will find some ideas for familiar-sounding programs in the next chapter. Something like Mastermind may not sound as exciting as Space Invaders, but it can be surprisingly addictive. Furthermore, it does not take too much effort to work out the core of the program (particularly since we've done the hard work for you!), and so you can concentrate on setting it out nicely, creating attractive screen displays and doing all the other 'housekeeping' which makes a game a pleasure to play.

Planning your programs

It is important to adopt a methodical approach when you write programs. Try to divide up the program into short chunks – maybe as little as five or ten lines each, certainly not more than twenty – which you can try out and test thoroughly. When you are sure that each short section works, you can then fit them together into a program that will work!

Manuals do not offer much help about learning how to program: they concentrate instead on explaining the key words and their uses. Programming is much more a matter of learning how to work out an algorithm – a 'game plan' – and how to plan the writing and testing in sensible stages. In case it's not clear to you how to split up a typical game, here are some suggestions.

First, work out the core of the game. Get the basic strategy right, and make sure the game does what you want it to do. Plan the core program as simply as possible. Don't bother with user-defined characters yet: use alphabetical characters in their places. Don't bother, either, with several levels of play, but stick to the simplest one. Test this simple version of the game thoroughly before you try to improve upon it. Take your time to get things right at this stage. You may enjoy the fancy parts more, such as working out the animation, but good displays for a poor game are no substitute for a good game. Make sure you have a good game at the outset – one that you will want to keep on playing – before going on to write a program around it.

Next, work out the basic display, or displays. What do you want the 'playing board' (the checkerboard, the maze, the ranks of invaders, or whatever) to look like? Plan out the display on plotting paper – graph paper, or a special 'plotter pad' designed for use with your computer (if you can't get hold of any, photocopy or trace the 'screen map' in your manual). Work out a static display first, and then the moving elements. Can you make your characters move so that they don't disrupt the background? Can you move them smoothly? You will soon learn what you can do with your computer's graphics, and start to tailor any grandiose ideas you may have to the level of your own programming skills.

You will find some suggestions for planning displays in the next chapter. Our finished programs show how we have dealt with specific points that crop up when we were working with the Dragon and the TRS-80 Color Computer – ways of coping with its insistence on printing everything in black on a green background, for instance. If you have a different computer, you'll have different strengths and weaknesses to worry about. We give an indication of what some of those might be, and make a few suggestions on how to handle different computers so as to bring out the best in them.

After planning the display, work out a title sequence. It makes a lot of difference if the game has a good introduction, to get the players 'in the mood'. Make sure that this includes a summary of the rules, and details of, for instance, which keys to press. Of course you may know *now* that you press 'F' for fire, and not the space bar, but, by the time you have a couple of dozen games on tape, you will have forgotten exactly what to do in each one. That is why you need to print a reminder on screen.

If your computer is short on memory, you can make this section a separate 'program'. On many machines, you can include in the title 'program' a command which makes the computer automatically load and then run the main game program.

Finally, turn your attention to the details. How is the score to be registered? Can you put in a high-score table somewhere on the screen? Do you want sound effects? If so, program them now. Try them out separately, first, and then add them to the main program. Make sure that the program tells you clearly when a player has won. You could, for instance, program a special 'You Won!' frame, complete with flashing lights and cheerful noises. Also, sort out a 'replay sequence', and so on.

You need never feel you've finished with a program you wrote yourself – or with a listing you've taken from elsewhere, for that matter. As you learn new ways to program, you can always go back to your old efforts to clean them up, perhaps improving their appearance, perhaps making them play faster so that they offer more of a challenge. That's what programming is all about.

Some common problems

You always have problems in writing a program. Everybody does. You could swear you've got it just right, but then the score appears right in the middle of the screen, instead of in the corner, as you intended; or the score doesn't add up correctly; or the game plays fine the first time round, but then goes bananas on the replay... the list is endless.

We cannot help you with the individual logical problems you will encounter. You will just have to sit down and work them out for yourself. Any good book on programming will give you some advice on testing and debugging. But we can point out some common problems in writing games programs.

One major problem is memory capacity, something we mentioned earlier. How can you make the best use of your machine's memory? Different computers organize their memory in different ways; they store arrays, for instance, differently. Magazine articles about your own computer will be helpful in giving tips on its peculiarities, and on how to get the best out of it. We offer, here, some general suggestions.

First of all, remember how much room high resolution takes up. On many computers, you will have much more room to play with if you stick to a lower screen resolution. For lots of games, simple, bold displays are good enough. Try the low resolution first; and only if you feel that it is inadequate, go on to the higher versions.

Second, remember how much room your program listing occupies. Make sure your program is logically set out. If you repeat any sequences more than twice (or even twice, if they are long), put them into a separate subroutine or procedure, so that you don't have to enter the statements twice. If you have space problems, prune your listing ruthlessly. Leave out the spaces and the REMarks: they all eat up memory. (But keep a well-documented version of your program written down somewhere, so that you do not lose track of how it works.) Not all computers free the memory space as soon as you cut down the program size: save and then reload the new version to see how you are progressing.

Third, think about your data. Arrays can eat up memory. Using single numbered variables (e.g., A1, A2 A3, instead of an array with three elements like A(3)) often helps. Long variable names – if your computer allows them – may seem fine, but they too take up memory space.

Finally, see if you can split up your program. An initializing program could not only provide a 'title page'; it could also, for instance, include your user-defined character definitions. Often these are not erased, as is the main working memory, when you load a new program. If your program contains two or more playing stages, make each one into a separate program. You can ensure by careful planning that it is clear to users how they should go from one section to the next.

Another major headache for games programmers is speed. You think you have found a great way to program a fast-action game like Breakout, but when you type it in you find that the ball staggers around at the speed of a geriatric snail. How do those professional programmers make things happen so fast? Well, often they use machine code instead of BASIC, for just that reason. If you don't want to imitate them – and yet want to write some fairly speedy games – here are some simple tips.

Take a good look at your program listing to see if there is any particular reason for the delays. Are you trying to do too much in a loop, for instance? Cut out everything that is not essential, or put it elsewhere in the program. Are sound effects slowing you down? Leave them out of the movement loop, and compensate with extra sounds elsewhere.

Again, high resolution can be a problem. Plotting shapes, and especially 'painting' them in, takes up a lot of time. Drawing and then moving low-resolution characters is far faster.

Many computers give you several alternative ways of getting much the same graphic effect. On the Dragon, for instance, you might either SET and RESET your medium-resolution pixels, or POKE in the values to the memory locations that control them. The comparative speed of the methods varies from computer to computer. Try several, and see which works most effectively on your machine.

Sometimes the computer's operating speed is slowed down to enable it to save and load programs more effectively. You may be able to speed it up by altering a suitable memory vlue. We have done this in some of our programs. POKE &HFFD7,0 speeds up the Dragon; POKE &HFFD6,0 slows it down again. (You must remember to do this at the end of the run!) If you are using a different computer, you will need to find out (from your manual or from a book giving you programming tips for your machine) the numbers that will do the trick for you – if it can be done.

That's enough of an introduction. Now let's look at some actual programs.

Some programs for you to try

In this section of the book, we are going to discuss in detail seven programs for simple games, graphics and sound routines. We will talk about ways of programming different effects and suggest how the programs might be adapted to make full use of the capabilities of different computers. Finally, we will be giving you a sample listing for each game.

The listings are written in Microsoft BASIC, and the programs are designed to be as general as possible, so you will be able to adapt them without difficulty to whatever computer you use – within reason, of course (there's no use trying to play the organ on a computer that doesn't have any sound!). They have all been tested, and will run as printed on the TRS-80 Color Computer with extended BASIC and the Dragon 32. They will also work on a number of similar machines. In fact, they are intended to provide ideas and to explain programming strategies, not to be polished programs, and so there should be no problem if you use a different machine. The important thing is to understand what we do in the programs and why, and then to adapt and improve them.

If you are familiar with our *First Steps in BASIC* book, you will recognize the version of BASIC we used there. We have changed the PRINT@ statements, however, to give the single number that the TRS-80 and Dragon computers expect. A screen map of these computers, on page 79, shows how these numbers fit on the screen. If you have a different-sized screen, you will want to modify our layouts anyway, and you may find our drawings of each program's main screen display more helpful in doing this.

Mastermind You probably know the game of Mastermind, although perhaps under another title – it has several. It's the game in which you have to guess a sequence of letters, numbers or colors, chosen at random by the other player (the computer, in this case). In our game, the items to be guessed are the letters A to G. Colors would be harder to program, and numbers can be off-putting to the nonmathematical.

The basic game

The computer selects, in lines lines 210 to 260, a random sequence of letters for the player to guess. You will see that it obtains a random number the required number of times, and then converts this to a letter from A to G by finding the ASCII code. CHR$(65) is A, CHR$(66) is B, and so on. It then builds the letters into a string, which we call S$. The next part of the program will manipulate this string.

The player has a fixed ten guesses. Line 310 sets up ten repeats of the 'guess a sequence' loop, and on each loop a string is input. The computer then checks (lines 350 and 360) to see if this contains the right number of letters.

If the player has guessed right, the program branches to a 'win' sequence on line 370. If not, the computer goes on to check each letter of the 'guess' string, G$, against the corresponding letter of the 'test' string, S$ (lines 380 to 420). The MID$ command is a neat way of doing this. If your computer doesn't have this command, there will be an alternative method of string handling; or you can put the letters into a simple array instead of a string.

If the two strings match, the computer tells the player so. If there is no match, it goes on, in the next section (lines 430 to 470), to see if the right letter has been given, but in the wrong place. The C array is used to indicate if a letter has been matched, and to make sure that the two sorts of check are not duplicated. The N array, together with the M variable, is used to hold the *number* of successful guesses.

The screen display

The player is not told which letters are right, only the number of correct letters (that's why we needed to use N as well as C). Lines 500 to 540 make the computer show the result of each guess. The display is shown opposite. In this version, a black square (CHR$(128)) indicates a correct guess, and a buff square (CHR$(207)) a correct letter in the wrong place. A com-

Mastermind – main screen display.
Black letters appear on a green background. The solid squares to the right of the letters guessed are black (for a correct guess) and buff (for an incorrect one).

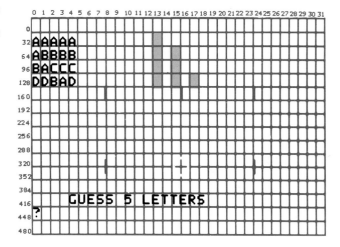

pletely wrong guess means a square printed in the background color. The sequence guessed is printed too – just you try playing the game without! – so that a column of guesses and results are built up.

While this display builds up at the top of the screen, the 'guess a new sequence' commands appear at the bottom. Once again, we have used PRINT@ to keep them in place. If your computer doesn't have a PRINT@ in its BASIC, you may find it easier to reverse the display: put the conversation at the top of the screen, and POKE the result sequence into the bottom half.

Changing the difficulty
It's much harder to guess five letters than four, or six than five. In this version, the level of difficulty (1, 2 or 3) refers to the number of letters to be guessed (4, 5 or 6). The D variable indicates the player's choice.

An alternative would be to change the number of guesses the player can have; or to let the player take as many guesses as he/she needs. Then you could rate the player at the end of the game according to the number of guesses taken. (Continued on page 84.)

Flowchart for Mastermind.

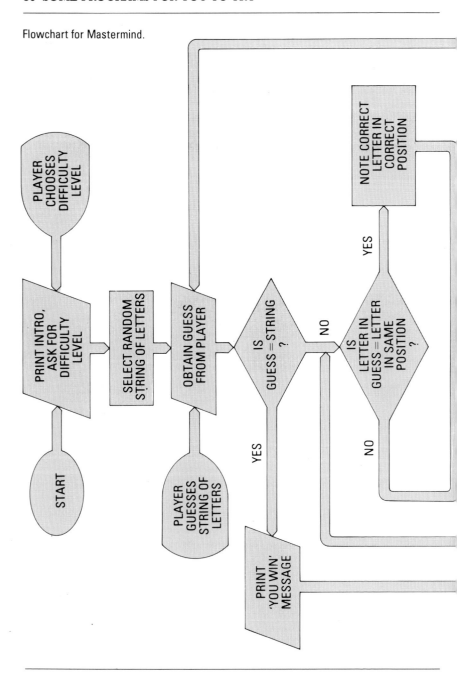

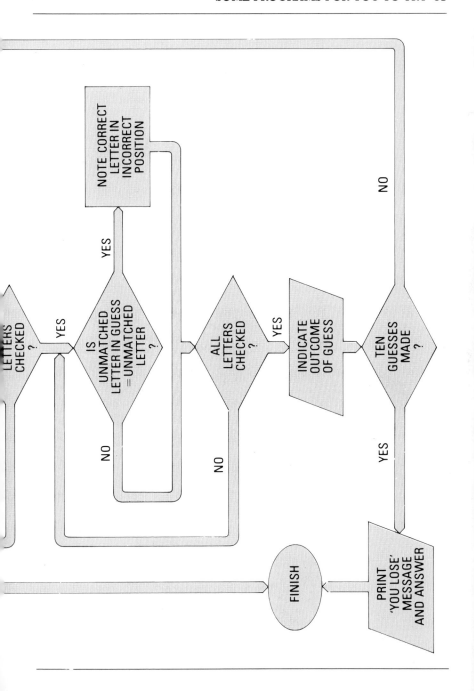

Mastermind _Program_

Variables _Used_
level of difficulty:	_D_
string of letters to guess:	_S$_
array to hold each individual	
letter:	_S$(6)_
array of check variables for	
correct letters:	_C(6)_
array of codes for printing marker	
blocks:	_N(6)_
loop counters:	
general:	_A,Y,X,B_
in counting guesses:	_G_
temporary variables used in	
building up string to guess:	_X,A$_
player's guess:	_G$_
counter for N array:	_M_
replay variable:	_Q$_

```
10    REM ***MASTERMIND***
20    REM BY MARGARET NORMAN
30    CLS: PRINT "MASTERMIND"
40    PRINT "I'M THINKING OF A SEQUENCE"
50    PRINT "MADE UP OF THE LETTERS FROM "
60    PRINT "A TO G.  YOU HAVE 10 TRIES"
70    PRINT "TO GUESS IT."
80    PRINT "EACH CORRECT LETTER IN THE"
90    PRINT "CORRECT POSITION WILL BE"
100   PRINT "INDICATED BY A ";CHR$(128)
110   PRINT "EACH CORRECT LETTER IN AN"
120   PRINT "INCORRECT POSITION WILL BE"
130   PRINT "INDICATED BY A ";CHR$(207)
140   INPUT "LEVEL OF DIFFICULTY (1, 2 OR 3)";D
150   IF D < 1 OR D > 3 THEN GOTO 140
160   CLS
200   DIM S$(6): DIM C(6): DIM N(6): LET S$ = ""
210   REM ASSEMBLE STRING TO GUESS
220   FOR A = 1 TO 3 + D
230   LET X = RND(7)
240   LET A$ = CHR$(64 + X)
250   LET S$ = S$ + A$
260   NEXT A
300   REM GUESS SEQUENCE
310   FOR G = 1 TO 10
320   LET M = 0
330   FOR A = 1 TO 6: LET N(A) = 143: NEXT A
340   PRINT@ 420,"GUESS ";3 + D;" LETTERS"
```

```
350  INPUT G$: IF LEN(G$) = 3 + D THEN GOTO 370
360  PRINT@ 448," ": PRINT@ 420,"NO, ";3 + D;"
     LETTERS": GOTO 350
370  IF G$ = S$ THEN GOTO 640
380  REM CHECK LETTERS
390  FOR Y = 1 TO 3 + D
400  LET S$(Y) = MID$(S$,Y,1)
410  IF  S$(Y) = MID$(G$,Y,1) THEN LET M = M + 1:
     LET N(M) = 128: LET S$(Y) = " ": LET C(Y) = 1
420  NEXT Y
430  FOR Y = 1 TO 3 + D
440  FOR X = 1 TO 3 + D
450  IF S$(X) = MID$(G$,Y,1) AND C(Y) = 0 THEN LET
     M = M + 1: LET N(M) = 207: LET S$(X) = " ":
     GOTO 470
460  NEXT X
470  NEXT Y
500  REM PRINT RESULT
510  PRINT@ (32*G),G$
520  FOR A = 1 TO 3 + D
530  PRINT@ (32*G+10+2*A),CHR$(N(A))
540  NEXT A
550  REM PREPARE FOR NEXT GUESS
560  FOR B = 1 TO 3 + D: LET C(B) = 0: NEXT B
570  PRINT@ 448," "
580  NEXT G
600  REM PLAYER FAILED
610  PRINT "   YOU HAVE FAILED"
620  PRINT "   IT WAS: ";S$
630  GOTO 650
640  PRINT "   WELL DONE, IT WAS ";S$
650  INPUT "ANOTHER GAME (Y/N)";Q$
660  IF Q$ = "Y" THEN RUN
670  END
```

Line-by-line notes on Mastermind

10–130	Introduction to program and on screen.
140–150	Obtain and check difficulty level.
210–260	Obtain correct number of random numbers from 1 to 7, and convert to letters from A to G.
310	Set up loop for ten guesses.
320	Set N counter to 0.
330	Fill N array with codes for green (background color) squares.
340–360	Obtain guess and check that length is correct.
370	Branch to win sequence if guess is correct.
390	Set up check loop for each letter in turn.
400	Set up array to hold each letter of check sequence.

410   Check single letter against corresponding letter in guess: if correct, change one location in N to code for black square, update N counter and mark check array. 'Blank out' letter in array so it will not be checked again in next part of program.

430–440   Set up double loop to check each letter against each letter of guess (not just corresponding letter).

450   Check all letters in turn: if correct, change one location in N to code for buff square and other points as above.

510   Print guess at top left of screen (below any previous guesses).

520–540   Print squares of appropriate colors across screen.

Starting and ending the game

This is one game in which you definitely need instructions, so you must include the 'title' sequence. You could improve upon our simple version by laying out the text neatly, using PRINT@ or PRINT TAB, or, if your computer lets you, using colored or double-height letters. Once again, the player automatically moves on from the introduction when he/she chooses a difficulty level.

This time we have included a 'replay' sequence as we promised (lines 650 and 660). This is about the simplest version you could have: only a reply of Y will cause a replay. There are lots of more sophisticated alternatives, some of which will be included in later programs. Notice that we use RUN to start the replay, not a GOTO statement. If you GOTO 'Enter level of difficulty' (line 140), then you also need to do some housekeeping, returning all your variables to zero. RUNning the program again does this automatically.

Other suggestions for improvements

There's little scope for major improvements here. Dramatic displays and noises are hardly the point of Mastermind. The appeal of the game – and it can be very addictive – lies in its simplicity.

You may like to change the colors to suit your preferences: a dramatic black background makes the 'check' squares stand out well. If your computer does not have color, then you can, of course, do a black-and-white version. Two different characters (perhaps a black square and an outlined square) could represent the two types of successful guess.

Countertake Countertake is another simple logical game. Since it is similar in general type to Mastermind, it is interesting to look at the differences when we come to program it.

Again, you may have already played a noncomputer version of Countertake. Played on the computer, there are two players, one of whom is always the computer. The computer displays a random number of counters – in our version, of one or two colors, depending upon the difficulty level you choose. The players then take it in turn to take away one, two or three counters. The object is to make your opponent take the last counter.

The basic game

The computer is not just setting the puzzle this time: it is actually playing the game, and much of the program is taken up with working out its moves. As this is a simple game, the computer can make good moves with no trouble. It will always beat a player who has a poor sense of strategy! To give its human opponent a chance, the program allows him or her to go first.

Two variables, NR (number of red counters) and NB (number of blue), control the random number (between 5 and 10) of counters of each color. On the lower level, only red counters are used. Lines 60 to 130 are occupied with finding the number of counters, and printing them on screen.

Lines 140 to 240 cover the human player's turn. The computer asks for a number of counters to take away, and for the color if there is a choice. The number goes into variable N, the color into C$. The computer checks to make sure the responses are sensible, and then branches to a subroutine to blank out the counters on the screen. This last is quite a complex task, which has to be done for both the computer's and the player's move, and so a subroutine is the obvious way to handle it. There is also another check in the subroutine. Suppose, say, the player has told the computer to remove three red counters and there are only two red ones left. In that case, an 'error flag' (E) will be marked, and the turn begins again.

Lines 250 to 390 consist of the computer's turn. It adds 1 to the number of counters, putting the total into M.

Once again, working from 1 upward makes it easy to use the neat ON... GOTO construction. Thus, if there are no counters left, M is 1. From line 280 the program goes to line 290, and reports a win.

If the computer hasn't already won, it works out a good move, and then branches to the subroutine to carry it out. Notice that these lines do not print on screen what the move actually is: the subroutine does that for both players (on line 1510). You may like to see, at this stage, if you can follow the logic behind the computer's strategy. If you can and you imitate it, you will find yourself winning regularly!

Finally, the program checks to see if any counters are left and, if it finds it has taken the last one away, congratulates the player on his or her victory.

One weakness of the program in its current form is that the game has to go on to the bitter end. When only one counter is left on the board, the computer doesn't resign right away; or if it is the opponent's turn and there is only one counter left, the player still has to remove it before being told he or she has lost. An obvious improvement would be to cut out this final move.

The screen display

As before, our version has the display of counters at the top of the screen, and the 'chat' at the bottom. You may find this inconvenient to program on a different computer, in which case it can easily be switched around.

We have used graphics characters once again for the two rows of colored counters. SETting and RESETting pixels would be an alternative, but the characters give a bolder display. There are no circular characters in the character set used by us. If, however, your computer has them, they would make the display more realistic.

Since the text on our computer always appears on a green background, we have once again set our display on green. Not everybody's choice, we know. Black, white or buff all look as good or better. Green squares blank out the red and blue ones as the counters are removed. The rather awkward-looking line 1540 does this neatly, starting with the right-most counter each time. An alternative, of course, would be to clear the screen and then redraw the remaining pieces.

Countertake – Intro

Notice how we've planned our PRINT statement so that no words are split at the ends of lines. This page is cleared when the player keys in his or her chosen difficulty level.

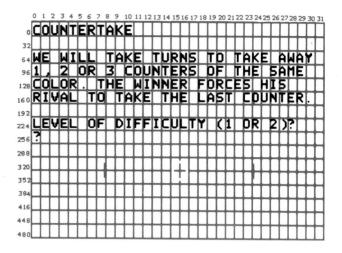

Countertake – main screen display

The counters are red and blue, the background green.

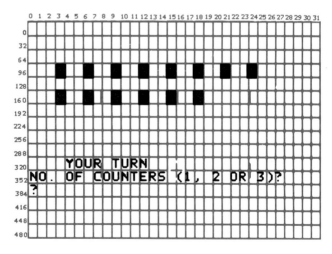

If you can define a 'text window', then that makes life easier. The bottom six lines or so of the screen could make a window on which the 'guess again' sequence scrolls up naturally. Meanwhile, the top of the screen would be used for graphics. You would need to use graphics commands, not character commands, to draw your counters!

Changing the difficulty

Adding more counters of each color does not really increase the difficulty of the game, as it only becomes interesting when there are only a few counters left. A good option would be to add a third row of counters to the two in our game. This is easily done.

Starting and ending the program

Again, a very simple 'title' screen could be jazzed up in any way your computer allows. The automatic replay sequence is a little more elaborate this time: any response starting with 'Y' will prompt a replay. Our computer doesn't have lower-case letters, but if yours does, you can use this version instead:

    IF   LEFT$(G$,1) = "Y"   OR   LEFT$(G$,1) = "y"
    THEN...

Other suggestions for improvements

There are no sound effects in this program as it stands, but you could add, say, a 'ping' as each counter is wiped out, or even a 'victory' tune and a 'defeat' tune. Once again, however, the simplicity of the program accounts for much of its appeal, and there is not really great scope for elaboration.

One feature our BASIC doesn't offer is integer variables, that is variables that can contain only whole numbers (their names usually end with %). By using these, you can make your program more error-proof.

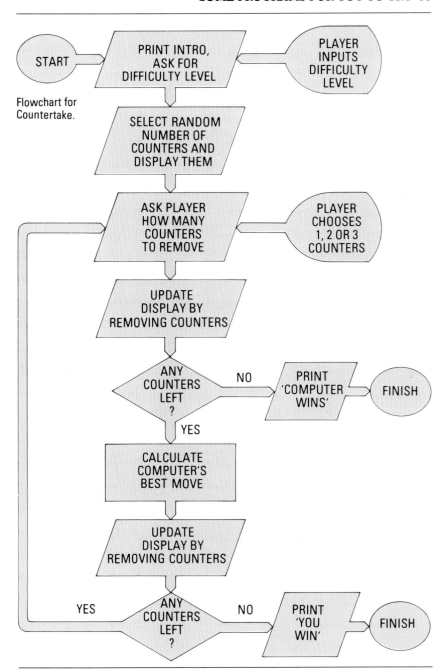

Flowchart for Countertake.

Countertake Program

Variables Used

level of difficulty:	*L*
number of red counters:	*NR*
number of blue counters:	*NB*
loop counter:	*X*
error flag:	*E*
number of counters to remove:	*N*
color of counters to remove:	*C$*
count used in calculating computer's move:	*M*
replay variable:	*G$*
delay loop variable:	*D*

```
10    REM ***COUNTERTAKE***
20    REM BY MARGARET NORMAN
30    CLS
40    PRINT "COUNTERTAKE":PRINT
50    PRINT "WE WILL TAKE TURNS TO TAKE AWAY"
60    PRINT "1, 2 OR 3 COUNTERS OF THE SAME"
70    PRINT "COLOR.  THE WINNER FORCES HIS"
80    PRINT "RIVAL TO TAKE THE LAST COUNTER"
90    PRINT: PRINT "LEVEL OF DIFFICULTY (1 OR 2)?"
100   INPUT L: IF L < 1 OR L > 2 THEN GOTO 90
110   REM PRINT RANDOM NUMBERS OF COUNTERS
120   LET NR = 0: LET NB = 0
130   CLS: ON L GOTO 180, 140
140   LET NB = 4 + RND(6)
150   FOR X = 1 TO NB
160   PRINT@ (160 + 3*X),CHR$(143 + 32)
170   NEXT X
180   LET NR = 4 + RND(6)
190   FOR X = 1 TO NR
200   PRINT@ (96 + 3*X),CHR$(143 + 48)
210   NEXT X
220   REM PLAYER'S TURN
230   LET E = 0
240   PRINT@ 325,"YOUR TURN"
250   PRINT@ 352,"NO. OF COUNTERS (1, 2 OR 3)?"
260   INPUT N: IF N < 1 OR N > 3 THEN GOTO 250
270   ON L GOTO 280, 290
280   LET C$ = "R": GOTO 310
290   PRINT@ 352, "COLOR OF COUNTERS (R OR B)?"
300   INPUT C$: IF C$ <> "R" AND C$ <> "B" THEN
      GOTO 290
310   PRINT@ 320,"      ": PRINT
320   PRINT@ 325, "YOUR TURN"
```

```
330   GOSUB 1500: REM DELETE COUNTERS
340   IF E = 1 THEN GOTO 230
350   REM COMPUTER'S TURN
360   LET M = NR + NB + 1
370   IF M <= 5 THEN GOTO 390
380   LET M = M - 4: GOTO 370
390   ON M GOTO 400,410,430,450,460
400   CLS: PRINT@ 448, "I WIN": GOTO 540
410   LET N = 1: IF NB = 0 THEN GOTO 420 ELSE LET
      C$ = "B": GOTO 380
420   LET C$ = "R": GOTO 500
430   LET N = 1: IF NB = 0 OR NB = 4 OR NB = 8 THEN
      LET C$ = "R": GOTO 500
440   IF NB = 1 OR NB = 5 OR NB = 9 THEN LET C$ =
      "R": GOTO 500 ELSE LET C$ = "B": GOTO 500
450   LET N = 2: IF NB = 0 OR NB = 1 OR NB = 4 OR
      NB = 5 OR NB = 8 OR NB = 9 THEN LET C$ = "R":
      GOTO 500 ELSE LET C$ = "B": GOTO 500
460   LET N = 3: IF NB = 0 OR NB = 1 OR NB = 2 OR
      NB = 5 OR NB = 9 GOTO 470 ELSE LET C$ = "B":
      GOTO 500
470   LET C$ = "R": IF NR = 2 THEN LET N = 1
500   PRINT@ 325,"MY TURN   "
510   GOSUB 1500: REM DELETE COUNTERS
520   IF NR + NB <> 0 THEN GOTO 230
530   CLS: PRINT@ 448,"YOU WIN"
540   PRINT@ 460,"ANOTHER GAME?"
550   INPUT G$: IF LEFT$(G$,1) = "Y" THEN GOTO 90
560   END
1500  REM SUBROUTINE TO REMOVE COUNTERS
1510  PRINT@ 340,N;C$
1520  FOR D = 1 TO 1000: NEXT D
1530  IF C$ <> "R" THEN GOTO 1590
1540  IF NR < N THEN GOTO 1640
1550  FOR X = 1 TO N
1560  PRINT@ 99 + 3*(NR - X),CHR$(143)
1570  NEXT X
1580  LET NR = NR - N: GOTO 1670
1590  IF NB < N THEN GOTO 1640
1600  FOR X = 1 TO N
1610  PRINT@ 163 + 3*(NB - X),CHR$(143)
1620  NEXT X
1630  LET NB = NB - N: GOTO 1670
1640  PRINT@ 325,"NOT ENOUGH COUNTERS"
1650  FOR D = 1 TO 1000: NEXT D
1660  LET E = 1
1670  RETURN
```

Line-by-line notes on Countertake

10–80	Introduction to program and on screen.
90–100	Get and check difficulty level.
110–210	Select and check random numbers of counters.
130	Skip second line of counters if difficulty level is 1.
220–300	Obtain player's choice of move.
230	Set error flag to 0.
270–300	Set color of counters to red if level 1; ask for color choice if level 2.
310–320	Screen housekeeping.
340	Repeat move if illegal choice was made.
350–500	Calculate computer's move.
360	Set working variable.
370–380	Work down to calculate end position.
390	Alternative moves for different projected end positions.
400	Result if player removed last counter.
520	Player's next go if game not finished.
530–560	End of game and replay sequence.
550	Any response starting with 'Y' or 'y' will cause replay.
1510	Print chosen move on screen.
1540, 1590	If player wants to remove more counters than remain, branch to error sequence.
1560, 1610	Print background color squares over counters to be removed.
1580, 1630	Update computer's data on number of counters remaining.
1660	Set error flag if illegal move requested.

Organ player   If your computer lets you play notes or sounds, then you can program it to act as a simple musical instrument. You write the program so that pressing a particular letter on the keyboard produces a particular note. Sounds easy? In practice, it can be quite tricky. Let's discuss how we might go about it.

The command upon which to base your program – as with so many games programs – is INKEY$, or its equivalent on your computer. The computer obtains a value for, say, A$, using INKEY$, and then checks to see what this value tells it to do – play a note, as in this case, or change the octave or some attribute (the length, the loudness) of the note to be played. That gives us a program sequence rather like this:

```
100   LET A$ = INKEY$
110   IF A$ = "C" THEN PLAY .5, 50
```

where .5 is the length of the note, and 50 its value. (Computers are not consistent about the order in which they put these statements, as we have already seen.)

That's fine where there is only one potential value of A$ to check, but it becomes cumbersome if you use, say, fifteen or more keys. Instead of putting a lengthy sequence of IF=A$ = statements in your program, you might prefer to put a 'look-up table' of note values into an array, and to read in data at the start of the program. The number of the item in the array could then be tied to the ASCII code of the key pressed, so that your statement would be something like:

    110   IF ASC(A$) >65 AND (A$) <77 THEN PLAY
          0.5,N(ASC(A$)-65)

ASC is the BASIC function that returns the ASCII value of a single-character string. Not all versions of BASIC include it, however. Our statement assumes that you are using keys with ASCII values between 65 and 77 – capitals A to M inclusive, in other words. The N array would contain the note values, so that if C (ASCII code 67) was the key to play note 99, then location N(67–65, or 2) would contain the value 99.

We don't do this in our sample program, because the ASCII values of the keys we use are so far apart that it is not worth it. It is a technique to remember, however, if you are short of memory, or if you want to use most or all of the keys on the keyboard to play different notes.

We have chosen to use thirteen keys to play a complete octave, duplicating C (an octave apart) at the top and bottom of it. The notes on the lowest row of the

Organ keyboard
Here are our thirteen keys. The first part of our program is taken up with choosing the colors of the keys and the background and then drawing the shapes on the screen. The rest is the 'play' section. How authentic the notes sound will depend on your machine. Music micro, please!

keyboard are the C major scale; above are the sharps and flats. The layout broadly resembles that of a piano keyboard. Nothing will happen if you press the wrong key (except a pause in the tune), but to remind you to press the right one, we have included a routine to draw the 'keyboard' on screen. We'll discuss that shortly.

In our BASIC, the notes can be described by letters, and the octaves by numbers from 1 to 5. You will want to convert C♯ and the other note names into the names or numbers your computer recognizes. You may need to change PLAY to SOUND or BEEP, and to change the syntax to match.

We have used the numbers 1 to 5 on the keyboard to select the octave to be played. In our BASIC, the octave defaults to 3 if one of these is not chosen. If this doesn't happen in yours, you will need to put a statement such as LET O = 2 ('O' for octave, of course) near the start of the program. (Try out several defaults an see which suits you.) If there is no separate octave parameter in your BASIC, then you will want to amend the note and octave statements so that the note numbers are increased or decreased suitably. If, say there are 48 numbers to an octave, so that one octave starts at note 53 and the next at note 53 + 48, then you might include this type of statement:

IF A\$ = "2" THEN LET O = 5 + (2*48)
IF A\$ = "3" THEN LET O = 5 + (3*48)

and amend the 'play a note' statements to:

IF A\$ = "G" THEN SOUND (length, not value +O)...

Notice, that pressing the ',' key in octave 5 will ask for a note out of the computer's range, and cause a program crash!

Using the VAL command, if you have it, you could cram all the octave selection statements into one complex one. The slightly unusual INSTR statement we have included on line 80 (which looks to see if string A\$ appears anywhere inside string O\$) is an alternative, neat way of combining the octave selection statements.

We have used INSTR again, on line 80, as a way of speeding up the recheck sequence if no key was pressed. You can omit this if your BASIC does not include it.

(Description continued on page 98.)

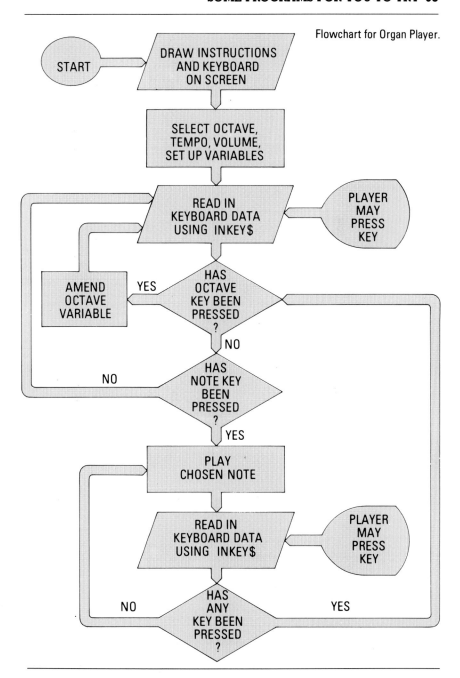

Flowchart for Organ Player.

Organ Player

Variables Used

delay loop counter:	D
general loop counter:	X
octave string:	O$
note string:	B$
key string input from keyboard:	A$
note to be played:	N$

```
10   REM ***ORGAN PLAYER***
20   REM BY MARGARET NORMAN
30   CLS: PRINT "PLAY THE ORGAN USING THE KEYS"
35   PRINT "INDICATED ON SCREEN"
40   FOR D = 1 TO 2000: NEXT D: CLS
50   REM DRAW KEYBOARD
60   PMODE 4,1: SCREEN 1,1: PCLS5
70   FOR X = 60 TO 160 STEP 20
80   LINE (X,40) - (X+18,100), PRESET,B
90   PAINT (X+10,50),0,0
100  NEXT X
110  LINE (100,40) - (118,100), PRESET,B
120  PAINT (110,50),5,5
130  FOR X = 50 TO 190 STEP 20
140  LINE (X,100) - (X+20,160), PRESET,B
145  NEXT X
150  REM DRAW KEY MARKINGS
160  DRAW "C5;BM 75,60;L8;G2;D6;F2;R6;F2;D6;G2;L8;
     BM 85,60;D20;R8;E2;U16;H2;L8": REM S,D
170  DRAW "C5;BM 136,60;L8;G2;D16;F2;R6;U10;L5;BM
     145,60;D20;U10;R10;D20;BM 175,60;D18;G2;
     L6;H2": REM G,H,J
180  DRAW "C0;BM 55,120;R10;D2;G2;D2;G2;D2;G2;D2;
     G2;D2;G2;R10;BM 75,120;D2;F2;D2;F2;D2;F2;D2;
     F2;D2;F2;BL10;U2;E2;U2;E2;U2;E2;U2;E2;U2;E2": 
     REM Z,X
190  DRAW "C0;BM 105,120;L8;G2;D16;F2;R8;BM 115,
     120;D3;F1;D3;F1;D3;F1;D3;F1;D3;F1;E1;U3;E1;
     U3;E1;U3;E1;U3;E1;U3": REM C,V
200  DRAW "C0;BM 135,120;D20;R8;E2;U6;H2;L8;R8;E2;
     U6;H2;L8;BM 175,140;U20;F5;E5;D20": REM B,N
210  DRAW "C0;BM 155,140;U20;F2;D2;F2;D2;F2;D2;F2;
     D2;F2;D2;U20;BM 197,130;R3;D1;L3;D1;R3;D5;L3"
     :REM M ,
220  REM PLAY SECTION
230  LET O$ = "12345": LET B$ = "ZXCVBNM,SDGHJ"
240  PLAY "T20V30"
250  LET A$ = INKEY$: IF A$ = "" THEN GOTO 250
260  IF INSTR(1,O$,A$) <> 0 THEN PLAY "O"+A$: GOTO
     250
```

```
270   IF INSTR(1,B$,A$) = 0 THEN GOTO 250
280   IF A$ = "Z" THEN LET N$ = "C": PLAY N$: GOTO
      1000
290   IF A$ = "S" THEN LET N$ = "C#": PLAY N$: GOTO
      1000
300   IF A$ = "X" THEN LET N$ = "D": PLAY N$: GOTO
      1000
310   IF A$ = "D" THEN LET N$ = "D#": PLAY N$: GOTO
      1000
320   IF A$ = "C" THEN LET N$ = "E": PLAY N$: GOTO
      1000
330   IF A$ = "V" THEN LET N$ = "F": PLAY N$: GOTO
      1000
340   IF A$ = "G" THEN LET N$ = "F#": PLAY N$: GOTO
      1000
350   IF A$ = "B" THEN LET N$ = "G": PLAY N$: GOTO
      1000
360   IF A$ = "H" THEN LET N$ = "G#": PLAY N$: GOTO
      1000
370   IF A$ = "N" THEN LET N$ = "A": PLAY N$: GOTO
      1000
380   IF A$ = "J" THEN LET N$ = "A#": PLAY N$: GOTO
      1000
390   IF A$ = "M" THEN LET N$ = "B": PLAY N$: GOTO
      1000
400   IF A$ = "," THEN LET N$ = "O+CO-": PLAY N$:
      GOTO 1000
1000  LET A$ = INKEY$: IF A$ = "" THEN PLAY N$:
      GOTO 1000
1010  GOTO 260
```

Line-by-line notes on Organ Player

10–40	Introduction to program and on screen.
60	Set graphics mode, choice of colors, buff background.
70–145	Draw key shapes on screen.
150–210	Draw letter on each key using hi-res line commands.
230	Set up string variables to hold octave numbers, permissible notes.
240	Set tempo at 20, volume at 30.
250	Check to see if a key pressed.
260	Check for octave selection and set if found.
270	Check for note selection and return to 250 if not found.
280–400	Play individual note (of present length, volume, octave).
1000	Check for new key pressed. If none found, replay existing choice of note.
1010	If new key pressed, then loop back to find new note chosen.

Getting the timing right

You will need to experiment with different note lengths in your program, to find one that lasts long enough to allow for the computer's next check of A$. In our BASIC, tempo and volume can be set once and remain until reset. We set them at the start of the program, in line 40. In yours, you may have to give the length and/or volume of each individual note, by putting an instruction into the 'IF A$' statements, like this:

> **130   IF A$ = "C" THEN SOUND**   (note, length, volume): **GOTO 1000**

One interesting problem is to decide what happens when a note finishes. Should you continue playing the same note until another key (even a 'dead' key with no value assigned to it) is pressed? Or should the program pause once the note has been played once? We found the program worked much better if we did repeat each note, and the sequence from line 1000 is a way of achieving that effect. Pressing a single key produces a sort of 'warbling' effect. Keyboards vary in their operation, however, and if your keyboard has an 'auto-repeat' on the keys, you may feel that this is unnecessary. (You might, however, find it necessary to flush the keyboard buffer before going back to check A$ again.)

More complex music

Are you thoroughly confused already? Well, if it's any consolation we're doing the bare minimum in this program. Just you try allowing for three or four different sound channels, and for envelopes to give your notes different sound qualities – let alone for coordinating the timing of notes so that you can play chords! Take a good look at the flowchart and program on pages 95 and 96, and all should become clear.

The screen display

It's not necessary to display anything at all on screen, except perhaps a message saying 'Press any key to play a note', or whatever it does! However, it adds to the appeal of the program if you have some sort of screen display.

We chose to draw a rough 'piano keyboard' on the screen, as you can see on page 93. Black and buff keys on a buff background (no white in our BASIC!) have the keyboard letters drawn on them.

To make the display look good, you need to draw the letters at larger than normal size. Ours are drawn using high-resolution graphics commands. An alternative would be to use block graphics characters to build up large letters; or to make each letter out of several user-defined characters; or, if your computer supplies one, to use a 'double-size lettering' command.

Drawing the keyboard is quite a complicated operation, as you can see from the program: it takes up lines 50 to 210 inclusive. If you don't want to adapt this section to a different computer – and that could be difficult if your computer does not have a good range of graphics commands – then what else might you display on screen? A simple alternative would be to draw a different-colored box on screen, or change the entire screen to a different color, each time a new note is played. You might choose to use particular colors for particular notes, or just randomize the selection each time.

Hangman

On, now, to a word game – the classic Hangman. There are lots of versions of this for home computers; ours is a fairly simple one.

The basic game

The aim of Hangman is to guess a word, either a word set by another player, or one set by the computer. In our version, the computer holds a list of ten words (in a DATA statement) from which it chooses one each time the program is played. You can easily adapt the program so that it asks you to enter words using INPUT instead, or look at the relevant lines (70 and 80) and change the words for different ones. We have included a simple check to ensure that each word is only selected once in a single run of the program. If the word has already been used, the location in array A corresponding to the word in array A$ is marked with a 'check', 1. When WD, the variable that determines the word to be guessed, is randomized, the computer looks to see if A(WD) is set to 1; and if it is, it repeats the operation.

The player has repeated chances to guess a letter, and the letter guessed is compared with the letters in the word, using the MID$ command. (You might like to compare its use here with how it was used in the Mastermind program, where we did something similar.) If the player's guess is correct, the letter is entered on screen, and the player has a chance to guess the word. If the guess is incorrect, a 'hanging man' is built up on the screen. When the man is complete, the player loses, and is told the answer.

An array, A$, is used to hold the words to be guessed. A second 'mini-array', B$, is used to hold the status of the player's guess – some blanks, and some letters already entered. Each location in this array holds only a single letter. The later locations are filled with blanks initially, and ignored if only a short word is being guessed. You may wonder why we didn't use a simple string variable here instead of an array. The answer is that it is simpler to update the array each time a new letter is filled out.

We use a check variable, SC, to hold the number of unsuccessful guesses. The subroutine that draws the

Hangman – screen display

The background color is green, the hangman and the letters black.

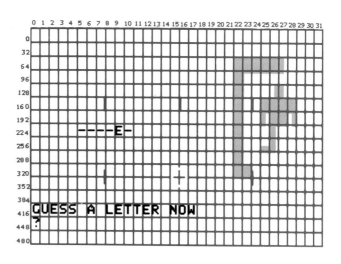

hanging man then branches with an ON...GOTO
statement, according to the value of SC. SC is updated at
the start of the subroutine, so that, though it starts the
program as 0, it becomes 1 by the time the first
ON...GOTO statement is reached.

The screen display
The screen is 'split' into three sections, which are kept
separate by PRINT@ statements. (You might arrange it
differently, once again, if your computer does not have a
version of this command.) One section displays the B$
array – the blanks and letters already guessed; one section asks for guesses at the letter or word, and the final
section holds the picture of the hanging man.

Our rather crude 'hanging man' is built up out of block
graphics characters. If you can define characters on
your computer, you will be able to produce a more
exotic version. The screen is cleared, and a suitable
message printed, when the player loses.

Starting and ending the game
The usual screen of rules introduces the game, and a
simple 'replay' sequence ends it. This time we do not
replay by rerunning the program since we want to
choose a different word to be guessed by changing the
WD variable which controls this. Line 840 does the
necessary 'housekeeping', resetting the check variables before the replay.

We haven't included a 'score' for the player, on repeated attempts, but you might do this if you wished.

Improving on the game
Some commercial versions of Hangman have made
strenuous efforts to liven the game up. One comes with a
complete firing squad instead of a gallows. However,
elaboration is not the point of the game, and a simple
version works fine. You might enjoy adding some short
noises to signal right and wrong guesses, and possibly a
longer tune (a suitable dirge, perhaps) when the player
loses. Another improvement would be to print the letters the player has already guessed in a row in an
unused part of the screen, possibly at the very top, with
our layout.

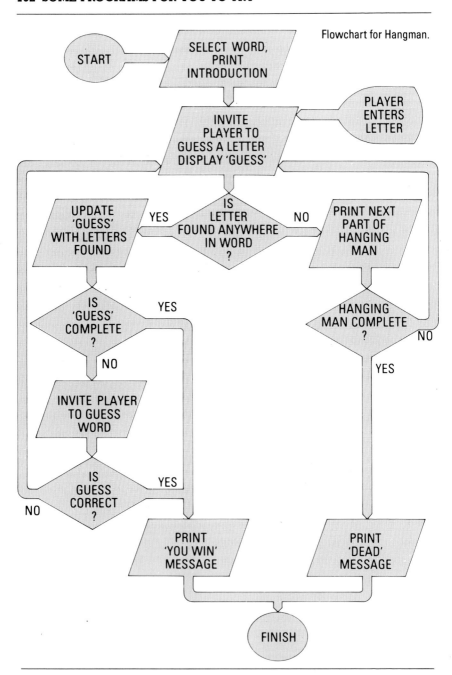

Flowchart for Hangman.

Hangman

Variables Used

array of words to be guessed:	A$(10)
check array marked when words used:	A(10)
array of letters guessed by player:	B$(12)
life lost/not lost on each guess:	LI
number of lives lost:	SC
player lost game:	D
loop counter:	X
dummy INKEY$ after introduction	X$
length of word:	W
delay loop counter:	DL
letter guessed:	L$
word guessed:	G$
check on word complete:	CH
replay variable:	R$

```
10    REM ***HANGMAN***
20    REM BY SUSAN CURRAN
30    DIM A$(10): DIM A(10): DIM B$(12)
40    FOR X = 1 TO 10
50    READ A$(X): LET A(X) = 0
60    NEXT X
70    DATA BROWN,UMBRELLA,WITNESS,CIRCUIT,STATUS
80    DATA WIDTH,QUEEN,ATTACK,ZENITH,BLANK
90    LET WD = RND(10): LET A(WD) = 1
100   LET LI = 0: LET SC = 0: LET D = 0
110   CLS
120   PRINT: PRINT "    HANGMAN": PRINT
130   PRINT "TRY TO GUESS THE WORD BY"
140   PRINT "GUESSING A LETTER AT A TIME."
150   PRINT "GUESS A LETTER NOT IN THE WORD,"
160   PRINT "AND WE START TO HANG YOU!"
170   PRINT "GUESS AT THE WORD EACH TIME YOU"
180   PRINT "GUESS A LETTER RIGHT.  NO LIVES"
190   PRINT "LOST IF YOU GUESS WRONG"
210   PRINT: PRINT "PRESS ANY KEY TO CONTINUE"
220   LET X$ = INKEY$: IF X$ = "" THEN GOTO 220
300   CLS: REM GAME BEGINS
320   LET W = LEN(A$(WD))
330   FOR X = 1 TO W
340   B$(X) = "-"
350   NEXT X
390   FOR X = 1 TO W
400   PRINT@ (228 + X), B$(X)
410   NEXT X
420   FOR DL = 0 TO 200: NEXT DL
```

```
430  PRINT@ 416, "GUESS A LETTER NOW  ";
440  INPUT L$: PRINT@ 416,STRING$(18," ");: PRINT
     "  ";
500  REM CHECK LETTERS
510  FOR X = 1 TO W
520  IF L$ = MID$(A$(WD),X,1) THEN GOSUB 1500
530  NEXT X
540  IF LI = 0 THEN GOSUB 1000
550  IF D = 1 THEN GOTO 810
560  IF LI = 0 THEN GOTO 420
570  LET LI = 0
600  REM CHECK TO SEE IF WORD IS COMPLETE
610  LET CH = 0
620  FOR X = 1 TO W
630  IF MID$(A$(WD),X,1) <> B$(X) THEN LET CH = 1
640  NEXT X
650  IF CH = 0 THEN GOTO 800
660  REM ALLOW GUESS AT WORD
670  PRINT@ 416,"GUESS THE WORD NOW";
680  INPUT G$:
690  IF G$ = A$(WD) THEN GOTO 800
700  PRINT "SORRY, YOU'RE WRONG";
710  FOR DL = 0 TO 500: NEXT DL
720  PRINT@ 416,STRING$(18," ");: PRINT STRING$
     (14," ");
730  PRINT STRING$(19," ");
740  GOTO 420
800  CLS: PRINT@ 320,"WELL DONE, YOU GOT IT!"
810  INPUT "ANOTHER TRY? (Y/N)";R$
820  IF LEFT$(R$,1)<>"Y" THEN END
830  LET WD = RND(10): IF A(WD) = 1 THEN GOTO 830
840  LET LI = 0: LET SC = 0: LET D = 0: LET A(WD)
     = 1
850  GOTO 300
1000 REM ROUTINE IF LETTER IS NOT GUESSED
1010 PRINT@ 416,"SORRY, YOU'RE WRONG";
1020 FOR DL = 0 TO 500: NEXT DL
1040 LET SC = SC + 1
1050 ON SC GOTO 1060, 1070, 1080, 1090, 1100,
     1110, 1120, 1130, 1140, 1150
1060 PRINT@ 342,CHR$(128) + CHR$(128);: RETURN
1070 FOR N = 2 TO 9: PRINT@ (32*N + 22),CHR$(128);
     : NEXT N: RETURN
1080 PRINT@ 87,CHR$(128) + CHR$(128) + CHR$(128) +
     CHR$(128) + CHR$(133);: RETURN
1090 PRINT@ 154,CHR$(138) + CHR$(133);: RETURN
1100 PRINT@ 186,CHR$(128) + CHR$(128);: PRINT@
     218,CHR$(128) + CHR$(128);: RETURN
```

```
1110 PRINT@ 185,CHR$(128);: PRINT@ 217,CHR$(133);:
     RETURN
1120 PRINT@ 188,CHR$(128);: PRINT@ 220,CHR$(138);:
     RETURN
1130 PRINT@ 250,CHR$(133);: PRINT@ 281,CHR$(140) +
     CHR$(133);: RETURN
1140 PRINT@ 251,CHR$(138);: PRINT@ 283,CHR$(138) +
     CHR$(140);: RETURN
1150 CLS: PRINT@ 320,"BANG! YOU'RE DEAD!"
1160 PRINT "THE ANSWER WAS ";A$(WD)
1170 LET D = 1
1180 RETURN
1500 REM SUBROUTINE IF LETTERS MATCH
1510 LET LI = 1: LET B$(X) = L$
1520 FOR X = 1 TO W
1530 PRINT@ (228 + X), B$(X);
1540 NEXT X
1550 RETURN
```

Line-by-line notes on Hangman

30–100	Initialize arrays and set variables.
110–220	Introduction on screen.
320–410	Print row of dashes on screen to indicate length of word.
440	Blank out 'guess a letter' message and letter guessed.
500–530	Check each letter of word in turn.
540	If no letter corresponds, go to 'hangman' subroutine.
550	If man is complete, go to 'replay' section.
560	If no letter corresponds, return for next letter guess.
600–640	If letter did correspond, check word for completeness.
650	If word complete, branch to 'well done' sequence.
660–700	If letter corresponded and word not complete, invite guess at word and check it.
720–730	Erase guess at word and 'sorry' message.
810–850	Invite replay and end program.
1000–1180	Subroutine to print hanging man. Lines are as follows:
1060	Base of scaffold.
1070	Upright of scaffold.
1080	Top of scaffold.
1090	Man's head.
1100	Man's body.
1110–1140	Left arm. Right arm. Left leg. Right leg.
1150	'Dead' sequence.
1500–1550	Subroutine to update B$ if matched letter found.

Dice

Dice is another game with a good graphics display, which may not be quite so familiar to you. The idea is to gamble on whether or not your die will roll a six. If it rolls any other number, then that number is added to your score; if a six turns up, your score drops to zero. The idea is simple, but the game works well, and with an attractive screen layout is enjoyable to play.

The screen display

The screen display is perhaps the best part of this game, so we will look at that first (it is shown on page 107). Since our computer can only print letters in black on a green background, we have tried to make that into a positive feature in this layout, by setting out lettering 'boxes' on a red background. The boxes are filled by printed blanks when no lettering appears in them.

The 'turn' box holds the player's score for each of his four turns, the 'total' box his accumulated score. The number in the middle at the bottom of the screen indicates how many turns have already been used up.

We're quite proud of the dice. Each player has one die and, as it is 'rolled', a sequence of different spot patterns appears until the die finally 'stops' at one of them. This effect takes a little more time to program than simple numbers in the dice squares, but it looks better. Block graphics squares in black or green (the background color – white, if your computer has it, might look even better) make the spots on the dice. Circles would be a further improvement.

The basic game

Each player has four turns, and we use the T variable to control a FOR... NEXT loop which is repeated four times. D indicates which player's turn it is, and that player then has as many chances as he/she wishes to roll the die, unless a six appears. R is used to trigger a roll, S to finish the turn. At the end of the turn (but not before) the player's total for the turn is added to his total score.

Rolling the die is a complex operation, and so we have put it into a subroutine. The subroutine first obtains a random number, and then prints the appropriate spots on the die. It does this five times, to simulate the die

Dice – screen
display.

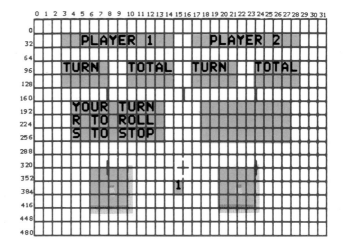

rolling over five times, and then pauses briefly on the
final side. This final value of X (the random die roll) is
then carried back to the program, and if it is not six is
added to the score, or if it is six the score is reduced to
zero.

The players
We looked at a game for two players before, Countertake, but then the second player was always the computer. In this game, the second player can be either the
computer or another person. The screen displays the
player's name, abbreviated, if necessary, so as to fit into
the boxes.

The program has two branches: one to cope with a
second human player, and a second to handle the computer's play. We will not discuss the computer's
strategy in detail: if you look at lines 710 to 730 of the
program, you will see that it is a combination of common
sense and random factors. This isn't a game in which
purely logical moves win, so you have a good chance of
beating the computer! (Continued on page 114.)

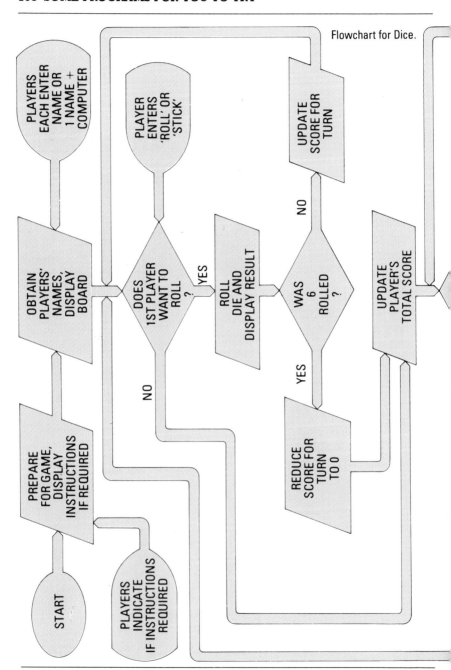

Flowchart for Dice.

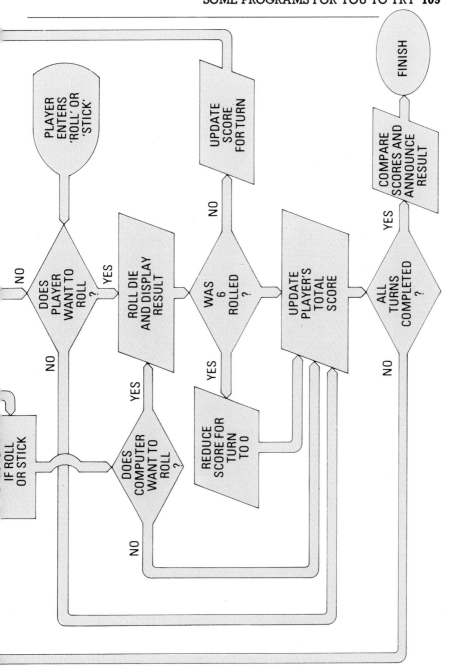

IF ROLL OR STICK

DOES COMPUTER WANT TO ROLL ?

YES / NO

DOES PLAYER WANT TO ROLL ?

YES / NO

PLAYER ENTERS 'ROLL' OR 'STICK'

ROLL DIE AND DISPLAY RESULT

WAS 6 ROLLED ?

YES / NO

REDUCE SCORE FOR TURN TO 0

UPDATE SCORE FOR TURN

UPDATE PLAYER'S TOTAL SCORE

ALL TURNS COMPLETED ?

YES / NO

COMPARE SCORES AND ANNOUNCE RESULT

FINISH

Dice Program

Variables Used

side of screen for each player:	D
seven alternative spots for each die:	N(7)
locations at which spots are printed: (2 dice x 7 spots):	SP(2,7)
general queries:	Q$,R$,G$
names of players:	N$(2)
loop counters:	A,B,C,K,N
number of turn being taken:	T
total score for each player:	T(2)
score for each turn:	RT
numbers rolled by dice:	X
computer's 'stick' point variable:	M
delay loop counter:	DL
winner:	W$

```
10    REM ***DICE***
20    REM BY MARGARET NORMAN
30    DIM SP(2,7): DIM N$(2): DIM T(2): DIM N(7)
40    FOR D = 1 TO 2: FOR N = 1 TO 7
50    READ SP(D,N)
60    NEXT N: NEXT D
70    DATA 359,361,391,392,393,423,425,372,374,404
80    DATA 405,406,436,438
90    CLS: PRINT@ 45,"DICE": PRINT
100   INPUT "DO YOU WANT INSTRUCTIONS (Y/N)";Q$
110   IF LEFT$(Q$,1) <> "Y" THEN GOTO 240
120   CLS: PRINT "THIS IS A GAME FOR 2 PLAYERS"
130   PRINT "(ONE OF WHOM MAY BE THE COMPUTER)"
140   PRINT "EACH PLAYER HAS 4 TURNS."
150   PRINT "AT EACH TURN YOU MAY ROLL THE"
160   PRINT "DIE AS MANY TIMES AS YOU WISH"
170   PRINT "A ROLL OF 1,2,3,4 OR 5 WILL BE"
180   PRINT "ADDED TO YOUR SCORE FOR THE TURN"
190   PRINT "A ROLL OF 6 RETURNS YOUR SCORE"
200   PRINT "TO ZERO AND ENDS THE TURN"
210   PRINT "THE PLAYER WITH THE HIGHEST"
220   PRINT "TOTAL SCORE WINS"
230   INPUT "PRESS 'ENTER' TO CONTINUE";R$
240   CLS: INPUT "ENTER NAME OF FIRST PLAYER";N$(1)
250   IF LEN(N$(1)) > 12 THEN LET N$(1) = LEFT$(N$
      (1),12)
260   PRINT "ENTER NAME OF SECOND PLAYER"
270   INPUT "OR 'C' FOR COMPUTER)";N$(2)
```

```
280   IF LEN(N$(2)) > 12 THEN LET N$(2) = LEFT$(N$
      (2),12)
290   IF N$(2) = "C" THEN LET N$(2) = "COMPUTER"
300   REM SET DISPLAY
310   CLS 4
320   PRINT@ (35 + INT((12 - LEN(N$(1)))/2)),N$(1);
330   PRINT@ (49 + INT((12 - LEN(N$(2)))/2)),N$(2);
340   PRINT@ 131,"      ";: PRINT@ 145,"      ";
350   PRINT@ 106,"TOTAL";: PRINT@ 120,"TOTAL";
360   PRINT@ 138,"      ";: PRINT@ 152,"      ";
370   FOR A = 358 TO 422 STEP 32
380   FOR B = 0 TO 3
390   PRINT@ (A + B),CHR$(143);: PRINT@ (A + B +
      13),CHR$(143);
400   NEXT B
410   PRINT@ (A + 4),CHR$(138);: PRINT@ (A + 17),
      CHR$(138);
420   NEXT A
430   FOR C = 454 TO 457
440   PRINT@ C,CHR$(140);: PRINT@ (C + 13),CHR$
      (140);
450   NEXT C
460   PRINT@ 458,CHR$(136);: PRINT@ 471,CHR$(136);
470   PRINT@ 392,CHR$(141);: PRINT@ 405,CHR$(141);
480   LET T(1) = 0: LET T(2) = 0: LET RT = 0
500   REM START GAME
510   FOR T = 1 TO 4
520   PRINT@ 99,"TURN ";: PRINT@ 113,"TURN ";
530   PRINT@ 397,T;
540   LET D = 1: REM 1ST PLAYER
550   PRINT@ 196,"YOUR TURN ";: PRINT@ 228,"R TO
      ROLL ";: PRINT@ 260,"S TO STOP ";
560   FOR A = 0 TO 2
570   PRINT@ (210 + 32*A),STRING$(10," ");
580   NEXT A
590   LET A$ = INKEY$: IF A$ <> "R" AND A$ <>"S"
      THEN GOTO 590
600   IF A$ = "S" THEN GOTO 640
610   GOSUB 1000
620   IF X = 6 THEN LET RT = 0: SOUND 20,5: GOTO
      640
630   SOUND 200,3: LET RT = RT + X: PRINT@ 132,RT;:
      GOTO 590
640   REM END OF TURN
650   LET T(1) = T(1) + RT: LET RT = 0: PRINT@ 133,
      "0 ";: PRINT@ 139,T(1);
660   LET D = 2: REM 2ND PLAYER
670   FOR A = 0 TO 2
680   PRINT@ (196 + 32*A),STRING$(10," ");
```

```
690  NEXT A
700  IF N$(2) = "COMPUTER" THEN GOTO 770
710  PRINT@ 210,"YOUR TURN ";: PRINT@ 242,"R TO
     ROLL ";: PRINT@ 274,"S TO STOP ";
720  LET A$ = INKEY$: IF A$ <> "R" AND A$ <> "S"
     THEN GOTO 720
730  IF A$ = "S" THEN GOTO 860
740  GOSUB 1000
750  IF X = 6 THEN LET RT = 0: SOUND 20,5: GOTO
     770
760  SOUND 200,3: LET RT = RT + X: PRINT@ 146,RT;:
     GOTO 720
770  REM COMPUTER
780  PRINT@ 210,"MY TURN"
790  IF T < 4 THEN GOTO 810
800  IF (T(2) + RT) < T(1) THEN GOTO 820 ELSE GOTO
     860
810  LET M = 15 + RND(10): IF RT < M THEN GOTO 820
     ELSE GOTO 860
820  GOSUB 1000
830  FOR DL = 1 TO 100: NEXT DL
840  IF X = 6 THEN LET RT = 0: SOUND 20,5: GOTO
     860
850  SOUND 200,3: LET RT = RT + X: PRINT@ 146,RT;:
     GOTO 790
860  REM END OF TURN
870  LET T(2) = T(2) + RT: LET RT = 0: PRINT@ 147,
     "0 ";: PRINT@ 153,T(2);
880  NEXT T
890  FOR DL = 1 TO 1000: NEXT DL
900  REM COMPARE SCORES
910  IF T(1) > T(2) THEN LET W$ = N$(1)
920  IF T(2) > T(1) THEN LET W$ = N$(2)
930  CLS
940  IF T(1) = T(2) THEN PRINT@ 235, "A DRAW!"
     ELSE PRINT@ 230,W$;" WINS"
950  INPUT "ANOTHER GAME (Y/N)";G$
960  IF LEFT$(G$,1) = "Y" THEN RUN
970  END
1000 REM SUBROUTINE TO ROLL DIE
1010 FOR K = 1 TO 5
1020 LET X = RND(6)
1030 FOR A = 1 TO 7
1040 LET N(A) = 143
1050 NEXT A
1060 ON X GOTO 1120, 1090, 1110, 1080, 1100, 1070
1070 LET N(3) = 141: LET N(5) = 141
1080 LET N(2) = 141: LET N(6) = 141
1090 LET N(1) = 141: LET N(7) = 141: GOTO 1130
```

```
1100 LET N(1) = 141: LET N(7) = 141
1110 LET N(2) = 141: LET N(6) = 141
1120 LET N(4) = 141
1130 FOR A = 1 TO 7
1140 PRINT@ SP(D,A),CHR$(N(A));
1150 NEXT A
1160 FOR DL = 1 TO 100: NEXT DL
1170 NEXT K
1180 FOR DL = 1 TO 200: NEXT DL
1190 RETURN
```

Line-by-line notes on Dice

40–80	Feed into array data on location of each spot on dice.
100–110	Conditional branch to skip instruction screen (useful for replays).
250, 280	Cut down names to fit into screen display.
320–330	Center names at top of each half of screen.
340	Prints blank green spaces below TURN headings.
360	Prints blank green spaces below TOTAL headings.
390	Prints green dice squares.
410	Prints black stripe down side of dice.
440	Prints black stripe along bottom of dice.
460	Prints bottom right-hand corner of dice.
470	Prints single spot in centre of dice.
510	Sets up loops for four turns for each player.
570	Blanks out messages for right-hand player when left-hand player's turn (needed for turns 2 to 4).
600	Branch to end-of-move sequence if stop is chosen.
620	Short low noise if 6 rolled.
630	Short high noise if other number rolled.
650	Adds turn total to right-hand main total: reduces turn total to zero; increases turn counter.
790	Computer's strategy is different on its last turn.
800	Computer's last-turn move if winning or losing.
810	Computer's move on 1st to 3rd turns.
820	As no INKEY$ function operates on computer's turn, short delay lets player see what number turned up.
1010	K controls five turns of each die (i.e. die comes to rest on fifth side).
1030–1050	Sets all spot locations to green.
1060–1120	Different spots turned black depending upon number rolled...
1130–1150	... and then black and green spots printed.

Starting and ending the program

Our introductory sequence is a little longer this time. It gives the player(s) the option of skipping the instructions, and asks for the player's names. If the name is too long, it is simply truncated. A neat touch might be to go back and ask for a nickname, instead.

The closing sequence has to cope with comparing the two totals, and seeing which is the greater. It then announces the result – which might, of course, be a draw. A straightforward 'replay' sequence completes the program.

Improvements you might make

Once again, there is not a lot of scope for improving this program. It isn't an elaborate game, and the program covers most of the eventualities. You might, possibly, like to add more sound effects, or more exotic opening and closing screens.

Artist We have already given you a program that lets your computer play tunes. Now, here is one that allows you to draw pictures. Artist links the computer's high-resolution graphics commands to INKEY$ statements, much as Organ Player did with its sound commands.

On our computer there is a wide variety of different high-resolution commands, and the program we have written lets the user select just about any option. Consequently, the 'work' section of the program is quite a bit longer and more complicated than it was in Organ Player.

The basic program

The flowchart on pages 120–21 outlines all the various choices we have allowed for in the program. The player can draw lines in any horizontal, vertical or diagonal direction; at any scale; in any color in the character set, using a background of any color, and painting in any color; and can clear the screen and start again without restarting the program.

As you may remember, our sample computer for this chapter offers two different 'color sets' in high resolution. There is a default foreground and background color in each set. The program comes up with this default selection, and the user can then change the colors if he or she so chooses. (It is necessary to clear the screen in order to get a different choice of background color.)

The INKEY$ commands are ordered so that the most popular choices come first, and the computer will respond quickly to them. The player is less likely to want to clear the screen than to draw a line, so this choice comes last! As soon as a command has been executed, the program loops back round to the INKEY$ sequence.

We have included an 'Instructions' command in this sequence, since it's all too easy to forget what the program does while it is running! Also included are some simple error checks, using INSTR again. If your computer lets you use integer variables, then keeping to these will make the checks simpler.

The cursor

One part of the program that may look confusing are lines 160 to 280. We will look in some detail at what these do.

Most computers have some form of cursor – a little flashing square or arrow that indicates where you are on the screen. This comes up when the computer is ready to do something new, but does not appear while a program is running. So, if you want to display a cursor while the program runs, you have to take special steps to enable you to do so. This section of the program is largely concerned with doing just that.

One problem that soon arises is that, if you 'draw' a cursor on the screen, it is likely to erase any drawing that has already appeared on the same spot on the screen! Some poorly written Artist programs will not draw lines from right to left because of this difficulty. We've got around the problem by programming a 'flashing' cursor, so that you have alternate flashes of the cursor and of the drawing underneath. Notice that this is rather different from using the 'flashing color' combinations offered in some computers' basic color sets. This flash is not a color combination flash, it is a programmed effect.

We have done this using the GET and PUT com-

The flashing cursor

In our program, line 160 draws a cross-wire on a 5×5 screen array (right). Line 170 GETs this area and stores it in a 5×5 memory array. X1 (below left). To print the cursor on the screen from, say, columns 10 to 14 and rows 5 to 9 (below center), the program GETs the drawing 'under' the cursor, in memory array Y1 (below right) (line 230), and PUTs it and the cross-wire image alternately on the screen (lines 250 and 270).

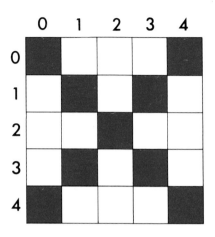

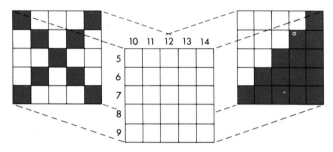

mands in our BASIC. The graphics details of the 'hairline' cursor are put into an array, X1, and the graphics details of the drawing in the same screen location into another array, Y1. The program then swaps them over, using a short delay loop to make the changes visible. Thus, line 160 draws the cursor, in the top left-hand corner of the screen (locations 0 to 4 in each direction). Line 170 stores it in X1. Line 230 does the same for the drawing, and lines 240 to 270 swap the two images.

GET and PUT, used in this way, are almost unique to our dialect of BASIC. If yours is different, you will need to find a different way of handling this problem. Some BASICs include an OVER command, which lets you superimpose images; some have 'exclusive OR' color handling, which has a similar effect.

Other points to notice

Notice how we have handled the instructions in the program. The main 'instruction set' is optional at the start of the program, and can be called up during it as we said earlier. The 'color introduction' displays samples of each color on screen (in low-resolution mode, in which they can all appear) to help the user to select a color set. Using the A$ string to hold the color choices means that the same program sequences can handle both sets of color choice, even though different numbers are used to describe the colors in each set (that is, in set two the numbers 5 to 8 are used to describe the colors; they are not treated as a different set of colors 1 to 4).

Line 210 may puzzle you at first. Why clear the screen each time the user fails to choose a new action? Doesn't that mean that when you draw a line across the screen, and then sit back to think what to do next, the screen will be cleared? No, it doesn't. CLS is the 'text clear' instruction; CLG is the 'graphics' version. Clearing the text screen with CLS does not affect the graphics drawings: it merely carries out a regular 'garbage run' on the screen prompts. If you cannot handle these by this method on your computer, you may need to use PRINT@ statements for your input on lines 400, 430 and so on.

Artist program – picture drawn on screen with color set 1.
(This illustration, and the one on page 118, show the design but not the full color range of the display, using tints we could truly represent all the colors on the screen.)

Artist program – picture drawn on screen with color set 2.

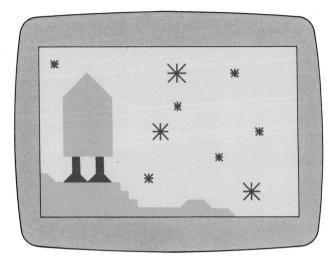

Notice that the 'scale' command provides an easy way of varying the speed to which lines are drawn. You can program in your own command to do this quite simply, if there is no ready-made 'scale' feature in your BASIC. You would treat S as a variable, and then, every time the 'draw' instruction is given, you multiply by the current value of S.

Our computer has both 'absolute' and 'relative' drawing commands. You can either give it the new co-ordinates to which you wish to draw a line, or tell it to go 'up' or 'down' by a particular amount. Relative instructions tend to be easier to use when drawing a picture, and the program is written so that the user enters instructions in this way. This is echoed in the graphics commands in the program, where we have again used the relative ones. If your computer doesn't have these, you can still give the user the impression of using them, by linking similar user instructions to program statements that update the drawing coordinates. This sort of statement would do the trick:

290   IF T$ = "L" AND X   S+1 THEN LET X = X–S: DRAW X,Y: GOTO 200

Notice that we have these statements in our program anyway, to keep track of the coordinates for the cursor position.

Starting and ending the program

There is no natural end to the program: it keeps on looping round until you BREAK it. An improvement, which would also end it neatly, would be to include in the program a 'screen dump' – a routine that copies the screen contents onto a printer or cassette or disk file. The program statements needed to do this, however, vary not only from computer to computer but from printer to printer, and so cannot be discussed in detail here.

Note line 750. "PRESS 'ENTER' TO CONTINUE" is a neat way of waiting until the user is ready, before clearing an instruction-type screen. It's a little shorter than using a dummy INKEY$ statement, and still only makes the user press one key.

Improving on the program

Some commercial artist-type programs include some highly complex facilities, such as 'fill' routines, which shade areas in different ways or create the illusion of extra colors. You may not aspire to these, but you will certainly want to adapt the program to make full use of your own computer's abilities. Adding a 'screen dump' routine, as we suggested above, is the only other major suggestion we can make for improvement.

(The flowchart, program and line-by-line notes on Artist are on the following five pages.)

Flowchart for Artist.

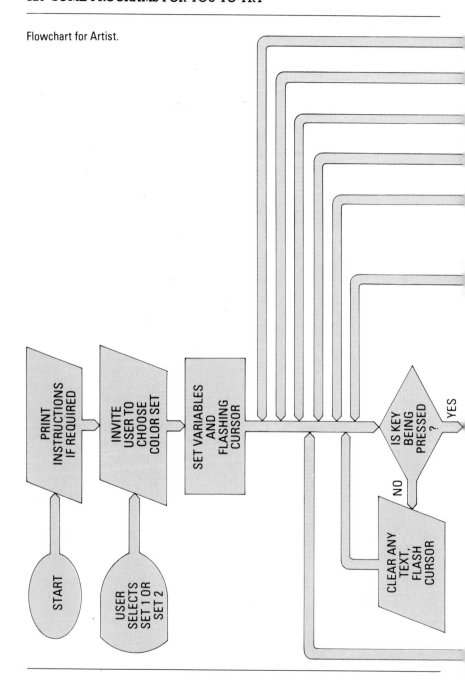

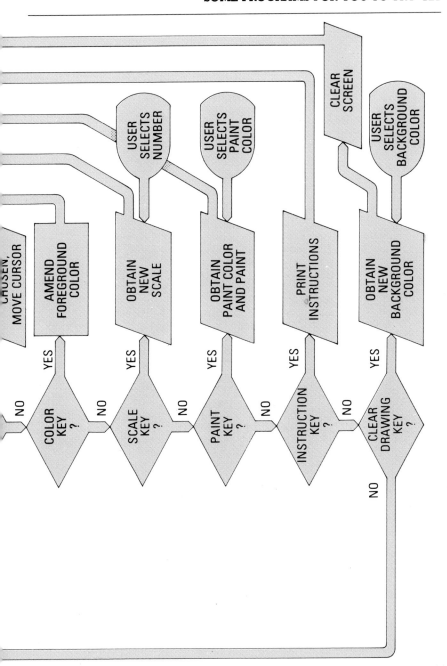

Artist Program

Variables Used

array containing cursor:	X1(4)
array containing drawing under cursor:	Y1(4)
coordinates of cursor center:	X,Y
general responses:	Q$
chosen color set:	Z
string containing colors in set:	A$
scale factor:	S
permissible choices in string:	B$
actual choice made:	T$
background color:	C$
paint and border colors:	P1,P2,P1$
delay loops:	DL

```
10    REM ***ARTIST***
20    REM BY MARGARET NORMAN
30    PCLEAR 4: DIM X1(4,4): DIM Y1(4,4)
40    CLS: PRINT@ 75, "ARTIST";:
50    PRINT@ 416,"DO YOU WANT INSTRUCTIONS? (Y/N)"
60    INPUT Q$: IF Q$ = "Y" THEN GOSUB 600
70    CLS: PRINT@ 34,"COLOR SET 1    COLOR SET 2"
80    PRINT@ 98,"1 = GREEN      5 = BUFF     ";CHR$
      (207);
90    PRINT@162,"2 = YELLOW ";CHR$(159);"  6 =
      CYAN      ";CHR$(223);
100   PRINT@ 226,"3 = BLUE     ";CHR$(175);"  7 =
      MAGENTA ";CHR$(239);
110   PRINT@ 290,"4 = RED      ";CHR$(191);"  8 =
      ORANGE  ";CHR$(255);
120   PRINT@ 355,"WHICH WOULD YOU LIKE?":INPUT Z:
      IF Z < 1 OR Z > 2 THEN GOTO 120
130   PMODE 3,1: PCLS: ON Z GOTO 140, 150
140   SCREEN 1,0: LET A$ = "1234": GOTO 160
150   SCREEN 1,1: LET A$ = "5678"
160   DRAW "BM 0,0;F4;BU4;G4"
170   GET(0,0) - (4,4),X1,G: PCLS
180   LET X = 2: LET Y = 2: DRAW "BM 2,2": LET S
      = 1
190   LET B$ = A$ + "SPCILRUDEFGH"
200   LET T$ = INKEY$: IF T$ <> "" THEN GOTO 280
210   CLS: IF Z = 1 THEN SCREEN 1,0 ELSE SCREEN 1,1
220   REM FLASH CURSOR
230   GET (X - 2,Y - 2) - (X + 2,Y + 2),Y1,G
240   FOR DL = 1 TO 25: NEXT DL
250   PUT (X - 2,Y - 2) - (X + 2,Y + 2),X1,PSET
260   FOR DL = 1 TO 25: NEXT DL
```

```
270  PUT (X - 2,Y - 2) - (X + 2,Y + 2),Y1,PSET:
     GOTO 200
280  IF INSTR(1,B$,T$) = 0 THEN GOTO 200
290  IF T$ = "L" AND X > S + 1 THEN LET X = X - S:
     DRAW "L": GOTO 200
300  IF T$ = "R" AND X < 255 - S THEN LET X = X +
     S: DRAW "R": GOTO 200
310  IF T$ = "U" AND Y > S + 1 THEN LET Y = Y - S:
     DRAW "U": GOTO 200
320  IF T$ = "D" AND Y < 191 - S THEN LET Y = Y +
     S: DRAW "D": GOTO 200
330  IF T$ = "E" AND X < 255 - S AND Y > S + 1
     THEN DRAW "E": LET X = X + S: LET Y = Y - S:
     GOTO 200
340  IF T$ = "F" AND X < 255 - S AND Y < 191 - S
     THEN DRAW "F": LET X = X + S: LET Y = Y + S:
     GOTO 200
350  IF T$ = "G" AND X > S + 1 AND Y < 191 - S
     THEN DRAW "G": LET X = X - S: LET Y = Y + S:
     GOTO 200
360  IF T$ = "H" AND X > S + 1 AND Y > S + 1 THEN
     DRAW "H": LET X = X - S: LET Y = Y - S: GOTO
     200
370  REM CHANGE COLOR
380  IF INSTR(1,A$,T$) <> 0  THEN DRAW "C" + T$:
     GOTO 200
390  REM CHANGE SCALE
400  IF T$ = "S" THEN INPUT "SCALE (1 - 15)";S: IF
     S < 1 OR S > 15 THEN GOTO 400 ELSE DRAW "S" +
     STR$(S*4): GOTO 200
410  REM PAINT
420  IF T$ = "P" THEN GOTO 430 ELSE GOTO 460
430  INPUT "PAINT COLOR";P1$: IF INSTR(1,A$,P1$)
     = 0 THEN GOTO 430
440  LET P1 = VAL(P1$): LET P2 = PPOINT(X,Y)
450  PAINT(X + 1,Y),P1,P2: PAINT (X,Y + 1),P1,P2:
     GOTO 200
460  REM INSTRUCTIONS
470  IF T$ = "I" THEN GOSUB 600: GOTO 200
480  REM CLEAR SCREEN
490  IF T$ = "C" THEN INPUT "BACKGROUND COLOR";C$
     : IF INSTR(1,A$,C$) = 0 THEN GOTO 490 ELSE
     PCLS VAL(C$): GOTO 200
500  GOTO 200
600  REM INSTRUCTIONS
610  CLS: PRINT "DRAW A PICTURE ON THE SCREEN"
620  PRINT "PRESS L,R,U,D,E,F,G OR H TO MOVE"
630  PRINT "THE FLASHING CURSOR."
```

```
640  PRINT "TO CHANGE DRAWING COLOR PRESS"
650  PRINT "COLOR NO.(1-4 SET 1; 5-8 SET 2)"
660  PRINT "TO CHANGE SCALE PRESS 'S' AND A"
670  PRINT "NO. FROM 1 TO 15, THEN 'ENTER'"
680  PRINT "TO PAINT, DRAW LINE IN BORDER"
690  PRINT "COLOR INTO AREA TO BE PAINTED,"
700  PRINT "PRESS 'P', NO. OF PAINT COLOR,"
710  PRINT "AND 'ENTER'"
720  PRINT "TO SEE INSTRUCTIONS PRESS 'I'"
730  PRINT "TO CLEAR SCREEN PRESS 'C', NO."
740  PRINT "OF BACKGROUND COLOR, 'ENTER'"
750  INPUT "PRESS 'ENTER' TO CONTINUE";Q$
760  RETURN
```

Line-by-line notes on Artist

30	Reserves graphics space in memory and initializes arrays.
70–120	Though main instructions are optional, color set choice appears each time program is run. CHR$ codes display solid block of each color.
130	Goes into four-color graphics mode: branches to select color set chosen.
140–150	Sets check string with allowable color choices.
160–170	Draws cross-wire cursor and saves it in array X1, then clears screen. G indicates graphics detail to be stored.
180	Sets cursor starting position and drawing scale.
190	Adds permissible instruction choices to color string.
200	Obtains input using INKEY$. If positive input, branches to line 280: otherwise, goes into 'flash cursor' routine.
230	Puts drawing 'under' cursor into array Y1.
240, 260	Short delay loops to make flash visible.
250	Gets cursor from array X1 and flashes in chosen position.
270	Alternates background drawing with cursor.
280	Checks to see if key pressed was acceptable.
290–360	If 'draw' instruction given, draw in current foreground color and update cursor position.
380	A$ is color string: this checks to see if new color choice has been made.
400	Checks to see if scale request made; obtains new choice of scale and implements it. (See how this is mirrored in instructions, lines 660–670.)
430	Obtains paint color as string, so it can be checked against A$; it is converted to a number on line 440…
440	…and existing cursor location color becomes border color.
480–490	Clears screen with new background color.

Breakout Now for our last game – a version of that old favorite, Breakout. For anyone who is not sure, that's the game in which you have to knock down a wall by 'hitting out' the bricks with a ball. The ball bounces back, and you have to 'field' it with your bat.

The basic game

It sounds easy, doesn't it? But, in fact, it is quite tricky to program. You have to move the ball, check to see if the player wants to move the bat, move the bat, or not, as required, check to see if the ball hits the wall, the bat or the bottom or sides of the screen, and act appropriately, updating the score, changing the ball direction, recording a 'miss', and so on. The flowchart on pages 130–31 shows how all these actions can fit together into a coherent game plan.

It is important to make Breakout a fairly speedy game. You will want to experiment to see how you can make your computer respond most effectively. We found that a good method of writing the program was to POKE the graphics character that forms the ball (a solid square in magenta) into the desired character locations. This also gave us a chance to include a program making use of PEEKs and POKEs in this chapter! If this doesn't work fast enough on your computer, you can PRINT the character as an alternative. Drawing it in high-resolution graphics would certainly be too slow.

Our method makes for a reasonable, but not super-quick, game. To speed it up for Level 2, we have resorted to speeding up the whole computer, using the special POKE command.

As PEEKs and POKEs may not be familiar to you, let us discuss them briefly before going on. By POKE-ing codes, you put them directly into given locations in the computer's memory. You can put a code into any read/write location, including the locations in which the computer stores your program, and many of its special 'working registers'. But be careful: if you do this to the wrong locations, you can cause havoc! A careless typing mistake could crash your computer. It won't do the hardware any harm, but to recover you will have to reset the machine, or disconnect and then reconnect the power supply. And so you will lose the program in memory. The moral? Always SAVE a program that uses POKEs, *before* you run it (and after proof-reading it as carefully as you can). Otherwise, a long spell of keyboard bashing may disappear down the chute!

The codes that we POKE are ASCII codes, and the ASCII extension into graphics character codes. POKE-ing does not use the CHR$ function, which normally tells the computer that an ASCII code follows.

Where do we POKE the codes? Into the section of the computer's memory that handles the screen display, of course. In our computer, that extends from memory location 1024 up to memory location 1535. It is likely to be different on your computer, so you will need to check your manual if you do not already know the addresses. Make sure you know how they correspond to screen positions, too. Not all computers (though most of them) number the locations row by row, just like the PRINT@ numbers we have been using elsewhere in the book.

PEEKing is a complementary technique, which gives you the code in a memory location. For the screen memory, it tells you what sort of character is in a location. We PEEK at the location where the ball is about to go (no point in PEEKing at where it is – there's a magenta square there, as we already know!) to find out whether it is about to hit a brick, or the bat, or a 'border' square. It's partly to make this practicable that we have drawn a buff border around the playing area. An alternative way of 'bouncing' the ball would be to check on the number of the location at which the ball is printed, and to act if it were a border location number.

Although the numbers of the memory locations we PEEK and POKE are not the same as the PRINT@ screen numbers, they can be – and are – treated in just the same way, if we add an 'offset' value to them. To get the equivalent of PRINT@, say, location 133, we POKE to location 1024 (start of screen memory) + 133, and so on. In this way, we can use loops and variables to manipulate the ball's direction and position.

As you can only PEEK at character locations, and not at the graphics screen (well, you can, but it will be differently set up), it is as well to draw your wall using graphics characters, not high-resolution commands. We have used the simple character shown opposite.

Breakout – screen
display.

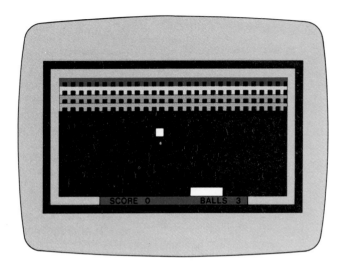

Graphics character
used to make the
wall.

One final point. We found that the game, as first
programmed, left quite a few 'loose' bricks at the very
end, and that it was difficult (our testers claimed imposs-
ible) to knock these very last bricks out. To clear up
some of the loose bricks, there is a 'random' sequence
which speeds up when the score goes above the 6000
level (that is, when the wall is about four-fifths
demolished), and which moves the ball sideways to
make it knock out two bricks at once. You may like to try
the game without this, and only put it in if you find it
necessary on your computer.

Using joysticks

There is no need to use joysticks for Breakout: you can
use INKEY$ statements, just as we have for the earlier
games in this chapter. But this version has been written
using joysticks, to show you how you program them.

The joystick on our computer (there can be two, but
only one is used for this game) returns two signals. One
signal gives its position: this is a number from 0 to 63.
The other indicates if the firing button is being pressed.
This can be read by PEEKing the memory location to

which the button inputs its signal. On this computer, a single location holds the signals from both joystick firing buttons. Its normal value is either 127 or 255, but it changes to various other numbers depending on whether either or both buttons are being pressed. ANDing its value with 1, as in line 280, indicates if one of these alternative values has been given.

A special JOYSTK command returns the number for the joystick position. The program lines that use this command (lines 1020 and 1030) have been written so that the speed (as well as the direction) of the bat will vary according to the position of the joystick.

Not all BASICs have a special joystick command. An alternative is to PEEK at the additional memory location(s) into which the joystick position value is read.

Though the general principles of using joysticks are common to all computers that support them, the exact numbers and statements we have used are peculiar to our computer. If you use joysticks, you will want to study our statements carefully in conjunction with your own computer manual's examples.

If you use INKEY$ statements instead, you may find it necessary to speed up your keyboard's response time, and to flush its buffer, if it has an auto-repeat feature. Your manual will show you how to do this.

The screen display

We have already discussed many aspects of the screen display, since they are so essential to the game. As Breakout games go, we feel this is a pretty attractive version, making good use of the computer's color, and laying out the score well. The buff border is a particularly good idea if your computer has a wide screen 'border', which you can make the same color as the playing area. Otherwise, it can be confusing when the ball hits the edge of the 'working' screen!

Although color is nice, it is not essential, as you will know if you have played Breakout on a black-and-white screen. However, you will need to be particularly careful in checking the ball location if you confine yourself to black-and-white characters.

(If you cannot get joysticks for your computer from the manufacturer, try an independent supplier.)

Changing the difficulty level

As well as speeding up the game on Level 2, we have included an option to choose the bat size. Naturally, having a smaller bat makes the game harder to play.

Starting and ending the game

The player does not always succeed in knocking down the whole wall by the end of the game. If he or she does so, an extra reward comes in the form of a special 'congratulations' sequence.

If you have tinkered with your computer's timing features at all, to make the game run faster, then it is important to remember to return everything to normal before ending the game. Besides doing this at the end of the program run (line 470), you may find it advisable to fit the necessary statements into an 'error' routine, if your computer offers them. Error routines, as well as coming up if an actual programming error occurs, are triggered by the 'break' key. A statement like

ON ERROR POKE &HFFD6,0: END

would suffice. In fact, the ON ERROR command isn't in our version of BASIC, so the example is a theoretical one. You would need to substitute your own computer's 'speed down' sequence.

Improving on the game

We are fairly satisfied with our version of Breakout, but as with all our programs, it is difficult to tell how well it will transfer to another computer. We leave it up to you to tailor our Breakout, and then to work on your own version until you are happy with it.

(The flowchart, program and line-by-line notes on Breakout are on the following pages.)

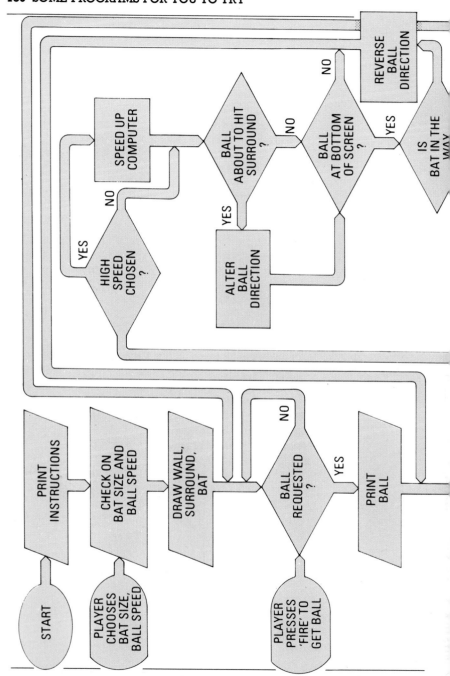

Flowchart for Breakout.

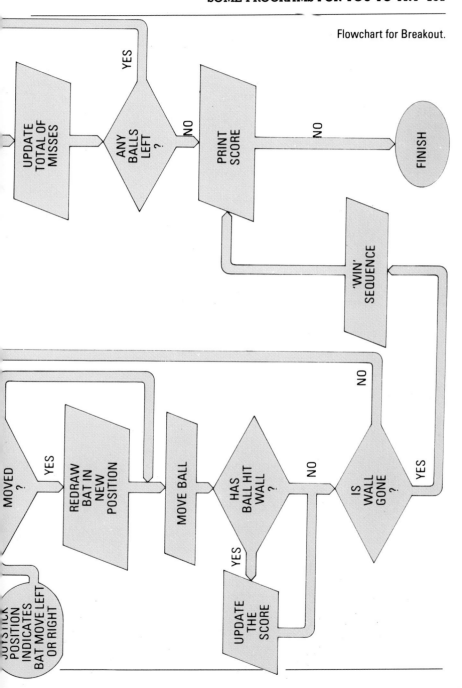

Breakout Program

Variables Used

bat size:	*BS*
speed of ball (1 = slow, 2 = fast)	*SP*
number of misses:	*M*
score:	*SC*
loop counters:	*I,J*
bat position:	*BX*
string to draw bat:	*B$*
ball position:	*BL*
direction of ball movement:	*V*
temporary store for BL/BX	*K*
code of character in new ball position:	*A*
random number:	*C*
color of screen in 'win'	*CL*
delay loop counter:	*D*

```
10   REM ***BREAKOUT***
20   REM BY MARGARET NORMAN
30   CLS: PRINT@ 10,"BREAKOUT": PRINT
40   PRINT "KNOCK DOWN THE WALL.  YOU HAVE 3"
50   PRINT "BALLS TO USE."
60   PRINT "MOVE THE BAT WITH YOUR JOYSTICK"
70   PRINT "PRESS THE FIRE BUTTON FOR A"
80   PRINT "NEW BALL."
90   INPUT "BAT SIZE (3-7)";BS
100  IF BS < 3 OR BS > 7 THEN GOTO 90
110  INPUT "BALL SPEED (1 OR 2)";SP
120  IF SP < 1 OR SP > 2 THEN GOTO 110
130  LET M = 0: LET SC = 0
150  REM SET UP WALL
160  CLS 0: PRINT@ 0,STRING$(32,207);
170  FOR I = 32 TO 448 STEP 32
180  PRINT@ I,CHR$(207);: PRINT@ I + 31,CHR$(207);
190  NEXT I
200  FOR J = 33 TO 129 STEP 32
210  PRINT@ J,STRING$(30,126 + (J - 1)/2);
220  NEXT J
230  PRINT@ 480,STRING$(5,207) + STRING$(22,143) +
     STRING$(4,207);: POKE 1535,207
240  PRINT@ 487,"SCORE ";SC;"    BALLS ";3-M;
250  REM DRAW BAT, WAIT FOR FIRE
260  LET BX = 10: LET B$ = STRING$(BS,239)
270  PRINT@ 449 + BX,B$;: GOSUB 1000
280  IF (PEEK(65280) AND 1) > 0 THEN GOTO 270
300  REM DRAW BALL
310  LET BL = 1194 + RND(10): POKE BL,239: LET V
     = 33
```

```
320   GOSUB 1000
330   GOSUB 1500
340   IF SC = 7500 THEN GOTO 600
350   IF SP = 2 THEN POKE &HFFD7,0
360   REM BOUNCE OFF WALLS
370   IF PEEK(BL+V) <> 207 THEN GOTO 400
380   SOUND 50,1: IF V = 33 OR V = -31 THEN LET V =
      V - 2 ELSE LET V = V + 2
390   IF BL < 1088 THEN LET V = ABS(V)
400   IF BL < 1440 THEN GOTO 320
410   REM HIT BALL
420   IF PEEK(BL+32) <> 239 THEN GOTO 440
430   SOUND 50,1: IF V = 33 THEN LET V = -31: GOTO
      320 ELSE LET V = -33: GOTO 320
440   REM MISS BALL
450   SOUND 20,10: LET M = M + 1: IF M <> 3 THEN
      POKE BL,128: PRINT@ 505, 3 - M;: GOTO 280
460   REM END OF GAME
470   POKE &HFFD6,0
480   CLS: PRINT@ 35, "YOU SCORED ";SC: PRINT
490   INPUT "ANOTHER GAME (Y/N)";Q$
500   IF Q$ = "N" THEN END ELSE GOTO 90
600   PLAY "T30V3104BAGFEDCO-BAGFEDCO-BAGFEDC"
610   FOR CL = 0 TO 8
620   CLS CL: PRINT@ 235, "WELL DONE!";
630   FOR D = 0 TO 100: NEXT D
640   NEXT CL
650   GOTO 460
1000  REM MOVE BAT
1010  LET K = BX
1020  LET BX = BX + (JOYSTK(0) < 10 AND BX > 0) -
      (JOYSTK(0) > 50 AND BX < (30 - BS)): GOSUB
      1100
1030  LET BX = BX + (JOYSTK(0) < 30 AND BX > 0) -
      (JOYSTK(0) > 30 AND BX < (30 - BS)): GOSUB
      1100
1040  RETURN
1100  IF BX > K THEN PRINT@ (448 + BX),CHR$(128) +
      B$; ELSE PRINT@ (449 + BX), B$;
1110  IF BX < K THEN PRINT@ (449 + BX + BS), CHR$
      (128);
1120  RETURN
1500  REM MOVE BALL
1510  POKE BL,128: LET BL = BL + V: LET A = PEEK
      (BL): POKE BL,239
1520  IF A = 142 THEN LET SC = SC + 100: GOTO 1600
1530  IF A = 158 THEN LET SC = SC + 75: GOTO 1600
1540  IF A = 174 THEN LET SC = SC + 50: GOTO 1600
1550  IF A = 190 THEN LET SC = SC + 25: GOTO 1600
```

```
1560 IF BL >= 1088 THEN RETURN
1600 LET V = 32 + (V = -33) - (V = -31) - (V = 33)
     + (V = 31)
1610 SOUND 100,1: PRINT@ 493,SC;
1620 LET C = RND(5): IF C = 5 OR (C < 3 AND SC >=
     6000) THEN GOTO 1630 ELSE RETURN
1630 LET K = BL + (V - 32): LET A = PEEK(K)
1640 IF A = 207 THEN RETURN
1650 POKE BL,128: LET BL = K: POKE BL,239: GOTO
     1520
```

Line-by-line notes on Breakout

90   Bat size refers to number of graphics characters used to draw bat.

100   If speed is 2, then machine is speeded up with special POKE on line 350.

160   Sets background to black and prints buff border at top of screen. Note that CHR$ function need not be included in STRING$ statement.

170–190   Prints buff border down sides of screen.

200–220   Prints four rows of different-colored graphics characters to make wall.

230   Prints buff border and green 'scoreboard' at bottom of screen. Final character POKEd in, not PRINTed, to stop screen from scrolling up.

260   239 is code for magenta squares which make up bat.

280   Checks to see if firing button on joystick pressed.

310   Sets slightly random initial ball position and prints magenta square which forms ball. V at 33 prints ball one row down and one column right on each loop.

340   7500 is maximum score. Special sequence rewards this.

350   Special POKE to speed up machine (specific to the Dragon). This is cancelled out again on line 470.

370   Checks to see if position at which ball will next be printed is buff border square. If not, 'bounce' routine skipped.

380   Amends value of V to change ball direction (see main text).

390   Check to make sure that ball does not go off screen.

400   If ball has not yet reached bottom of screen, it is reprinted one row lower.

420   Checks to see if square immediately below ball is part of magenta bat. If not, branches to 'ball missed' sequence.

430   Same short 'beep' as occurs when ball hits screen sides is sounded when ball hits bat.

450   Longer, lower beep signals miss. Score updated and new ball

	prepared unless all balls have been used.
470	POKE to ensure that machine is operating at normal speed.
600	Short congratulatory tune (fast downward scale) if player has demolished whole wall.
610–640	Congratulation sequence also includes screen flashing in different colors.
1010	Stores bat position temporarily in variable K.
1020–1110	Checks to find value returned by joystick, which is between 0 and 63, and moves bat accordingly. See main text.
1510	Blanks out former ball with black square (code 128). Adds movement variable to ball position variable. Puts code for new square into A variable. Prints ball at this new position.
1520–1550	Adds suitable amounts to score, depending upon value of brick player has knocked out of wall.
1560	Returns to main program if ball is at top of screen.
1600	Reverses direction of ball.
1610	Short high beep to signal hit: increases score.
1620	Random element which speeds toward end of game (when score is over 6000) to help knock out final bricks.
1630	If random sequence triggered, program checks value of square immediately above ball.
1640	Aborts sequence if square above ball is part of the buff border.
1650	Moves ball one row upward.

8 Buying prewritten programs

Even if you are learning to write your own programs, you will still want to buy some professionally written ones. Here are some hints on how to go about it.

Forms in which programs come

Programs come in five main forms:
cartridges and ROM chips
cassettes and disks
listings in magazines and books
'telesoftware', broadcast by a teletext system and electronically transmitted through a network like the UK's Micronet.

Cartridges and ROMs are expensive to develop, and so they are only produced by major software houses who expect to sell a large number of copies of a program. As a result, the quality is generally, though not always, high. The cost is also high – sometimes ridiculously so, considering that the actual cartridges and ROMs are not expensive to manufacture in quantity. However, programs in this form are easy to use, and robust. They are also hard to copy, which is one reason for the trend toward them!

Programs on cassette and disk are easy to produce, and there are many small and cheap software houses producing them – and many large and reputable companies, too. Disk-based programs are simple to use, and quick to access. Cassettes are slow, but if you do not have a disk drive, you will be resigned to that by now! Both forms of program are easily damaged, and you must keep them carefully. If you can, make a backup copy. If the listing is 'protected', and you find that you can't do so, then the software producer should be willing to exchange your copy if it fails in use.

Listings in magazines and books are the least convenient form of program – it's you who has to type them into your machine! (Once you've typed a program in once, you will, of course, want to save it on a cassette or disk.) It is also you who has to 'debug' the program if you make any typing errors, or if – as quite often happens – there are bugs in the printed listing. The listings are generally in BASIC or another high-level language; the programs often won't compare in speed with a machine-code version. Typing in listings is, however, a good way of building up a program library cheaply and fairly quickly.

Telesoftware and software sold through networks are both new developments, which seem at present to be taking off well. At the moment, the networked software on offer is not particularly cheap: you have to pay a membership fee, as well as buying the programs you select. However, if the volume of users increases, the price may come down. Telesoftware is heavily slanted to educational users; networked software is more general. Loading the software is easy in theory, but in practice it may take a while for you to get the hang of it.

Finding software for your computer

Whichever form your software comes in, it is essential to make sure, before buying, that it will run on your computer. Check not only which computer model the program was designed for, but also the need for extras (more memory? joysticks?), and the version of the operating system, if you know that there are several different ones for your computer. If in doubt, ask before you buy. If you plan to adapt a listing, such as any of those we gave in the last chapter, look through to see what commands are used. Does your BASIC use them, or do you know how to achieve the same effect using different commands? Make sure you know what lines of the program do what, and where to adapt it to allow for, for instance, a different screen size.

Adapting programs is not always easy, and we do not advise you to try it for very machine-specific listings, or for any long programs. It is not practical to plan to adapt any form of program other than printed listings.

The wide availability of software is a strong selling-point for popular computers. Less popular and very new machines are not so well supported. Don't believe the computer advertisements: look to see if you can find any programs, before choosing a computer! Buying a brand-new computer for which programs have not yet been developed may mean a wait of six months or more before a selection trickles onto the market. Buying an unpopular computer will mean that few programs will ever be available.

The cost of programs

How much should you pay? That depends on the type of program, and on your computer. Business-oriented programs can be much more expensive than games programs. Cartridges and ROMs generally cost more than tapes or disks. The going price for games on one computer might, unaccountably be almost twice as much as it is for games on a different machine. Look around to see what is being charged. You may rightly be wary of 'incredible bargains', but the most expensive programs are not always the best.

Where to buy

Increasingly, programs are being sold over the counter in computer stores, but some are still available only by mail order. Buying by mail order, however, may involve some delay between paying your money and receiving the goods. All computer magazines contain lots of advertisements for programs. You should read them.

Who to buy from

More large firms are entering the games market, but there are still plenty of tiny ones, too. Quality, like price, varies enormously, and the big firms have little, if any, edge in reputation over the small. Some of the most admired programs are the only product of one-man bands! And though you may think that the big names mean professional resources, often the large companies buy software from amateurs. Just read those ads for programmers. It is people like you who are replying to them, and often the material they submit is no better than you could produce! (Apologies, if you are a professional yourself.) Do you really want to pay through the nose for a couple of programs like those listed in this book? Until the market 'shakes out', it is advisable to tread cautiously and always to read reviews of programs before buying.

The review market is certainly booming. Most magazines now review games programs while, until recently, only the specialist 'gamer' ones did. If you are not an expert game player, though, read the reviews carefully. One person's exciting, fast-moving game may be almost totally unplayable to another.

Take a good look at the program packaging before you buy, and at the presentation of advertisements. Often – but again, not always – a poorly produced pack, and an advert full of spelling mistakes, mean sloppy programming too.

Computer clubs

By 'computer clubs', we mean genuine user groups, not the pseudo-clubs set up by software salesmen. If you join a computer club you will meet other people using your type of computer, and be able to exchange ideas with them. But resist the temptation to pirate the programs they have bought! On the other hand, feel free to swap the listings you have developed yourself with those other members have developed. Also, try out their games to see which ones are worth buying yourself, and copy onto tape or disk the listings they have typed in from books and magazines. Make sure you take advantage of any bulk-purchase schemes the club has managed to set up.

Computer magazines

New magazines are appearing almost every week, so it is difficult to give you an up-to-date list of recommendations. Look at your local news stand, and check out, in particular, those that contain listings for your computer. But don't ignore the others entirely. They are certainly not a waste of money, and often contain useful articles and tips. It's also well worth reading the software and hardware ads, the program reviews and other features. You will soon discover which magazines publish carefully checked, well-documented, and generally *good* programs; and which other ones seem to publish everything their readers submit, whether good, indifferent or just plain awful.

Are you itching to get your own efforts in print? By trying out the published listings, you will soon get a good idea of the standard that is expected. Virtually all magazines will accept unsolicited program listings from their readers, and they will pay you a small fee if your program is published.

Glossary

Algorithm A precise, step-by-step procedure for solving a problem or planning a computer program.

Array General term for an ordered set of locations, variable memory locations, or locations on the screen.

ASCII American Standard Code for Information Interchange. A code whch assigns a number to each letter, number and keyboard character, and often to graphics characters too. The CHR$ function is used to give ASCII codes in BASIC programs.

BASIC The high-level language in which the programs in this book are written.

Binary A way of coding information, or carrying out arithmetic, using only the two digits 0 and 1.

Bit A single digit (0 or 1) used by a computer. (Binary digIT.)

Bug An error in a program.

Byte Normally a group of eight bits, a single computer 'word'.

Cartridge Computer add-on. A packaged circuit which can be slotted into the computer casing, to fix on to the main circuitry. Normally contains a program in read-only form, or a block of random access memory.

Chip An electronic circuit in integrated form: a major component of microcomputers.

Cursor Small 'marker' on the screen which indicates where the next output will appear.

Debug To correct a program and make it run correctly.

Disk drive The machine that 'plays' either hard or floppy computer disks enabling information to be read from or written on to the disks.

Floppy disk Flexible disk of magnetic material used to store data, a more convenient alternative to cassette tapes.

Hexadecimal Arithmetic system using the ten digits 0 to 9, and the letters A to F. Used by machine code programmers, and often in defining computer characters.

High-level language An easy-to-use computer language such as BASIC, COMAL, Pascal or Forth.

K Kilobyte: 1024 bytes (often approximated to 1000). A unit used for measuring a computer's memory size.

Machine code The computer's own language, in which programs can be written. Efficient, but can be hard to write.

Memory The electronic data storage locations in a computer.

Mode Term often used to describe different ways of handling a video screen.

Page Distinct section of computer memory that might be used to store data on a screen image.

Pixel The smallest addressable element of the computer screen in any one mode.

RAM Random-access, or read-write internal computer memory.

Register Special set of computer memory locations, used to control a particular function of the computer.

ROM Read-only memory, used by the manufacturer for storing unchanging information in the computer.

Software General word for computer programs and utilities.

Teletext The broadcasting of digital information. 'Telesoftware' are computer programs broadcast via teletext.

Video screen A screen used for computer output: either a television screen, or a special monitor.

Index

Acknowledgments

Series Editor   Lionel Bender
Art Editor   Patrick Nugent

Editor   Mike March
Designer   Sue Rawkins

Production Editor   Fred Gill
Art Director   Debbie MacKinnon

Illustrators
Hayward and Martin Ltd
Radius
David Whelan
The Communication Studio

Jacket photograph
Martin Burke

Photographic services
Negs Photographic Ltd

Typesetting
Facet Filmsetting Ltd
Southend-on-Sea, Essex

Reproduction
Facet Filmsetting Ltd and
David Brin Ltd, London EC1

In preparing this book, and trying to plan programs which could easily be widely adapted, the following six computers were used: Commodore 64, Dragon 32, Grundy NewBrain, Timex 2000/Sinclair Spectrum, TRS-80 Color Computer and Torch (the machine on which the book was written), which uses BBC Microsystem BASIC.

The authors would like to thank Grundy Business Systems Ltd. for the loan of the NewBrain computer they used in developing this book; Tandy Corporation (UK) for the loan of a TRS-80 Color Computer; and Dragon Data Ltd. and Commodore Business Machines Inc. for providing additional data on the Dragon 32 and Commodore 64 respectively. Thanks, too, to those involved in discussions about the book, and providing information for it, including the Paterson family and Mike Smith. Finally, the authors give special thanks to Margaret Norman, who wrote most of the programs in Chapter 7.

Frances Lincoln would like to thank John Pallot at The Communication Studio, 6 Paddington Street, London W1M 3LA, for producing the computer screen images included in the book, and Curry's Micro C, 21 Hampstead Road, London NW1, for supplying various items of hardware used as reference for illustrations and for the jacket photograph for the book. The index was compiled by Anne Hardy.

Special thanks are given to Richard Pawson, Editor of *Microcomputer Printout* and *Business Micro* magazines, who acted as Series Consultant.